# The Norsk Høstfest:

## A celebration of ethnic food and ethnic identity

# SIL International®
## Publications in Ethnography 41

Publications in Ethnography (formerly International Museum of Cultures Series) focuses on cultural studies of minority peoples of various parts of the world. While most volumes are authored by members of SIL International who have done ethnologic research in a minority language, suitable works by others will also occasionally form part of the series.

**Series Editor**
G. Tomas Woodward

**Volume Editor**
Doris Blood

**Production Staff**
Bonnie Brown, Managing Editor
Judy Benjamin, Compositor
Barb Alber, Cover Design

# The Norsk Høstfest:
## A celebration of ethnic food and ethnic identity

Paul Thomas Emch

SIL International®
Dallas, Texas

© 2011 by SIL International®
Library of Congress Catalog No: 2010940449
ISBN: 978-1-55671-265-4
ISSN: 0-0895-9897

Printed in the United States of America

Copies of this and other publications of SIL International® may be obtained from

SIL International Publications
7500 West Camp Wisdom Road
Dallas, TX 75236-5699

Voice: 972-708-7404
Fax: 972-708-7363
Email: academic_books@sil.org
Internet: http://www.ethnologue.com

# Foreword

About six years ago, Paul Emch walked into my office at North Dakota State University and introduced himself. I liked Paul the minute I met him, largely due to his easy-going style and confident smile. Although I introduced myself as "Doctor Kloberdanz," Paul responded by calling me "Tim." I then asked if he was from western North Dakota (where formal titles like "Doctor" and "Professor" are less frequently used than in the eastern part of the state). Paul explained that he indeed was from western North Dakota and had grown up in the Belfield area. He expressed an unusually strong interest in anthropology and asked if I would help him in the capacity of an academic advisor at NDSU. I agreed and for the next two years, Paul and I worked together on a number of anthropology classes and research projects. I was constantly impressed by Paul's work ethic, positive outlook, and his ability to connect with people of all backgrounds.

As a result of taking one of my "Cultural Dynamics" seminars that focused on festivals and festive life, Paul became very interested in the Norsk Høstfest that is held each October in Minot, North Dakota. He opted to do his seminar paper on the event and later decided to expand the material into a thesis project for his Master's degree. Paul never wavered in his commitment to turn out a top-notch and scholarly treatment of one of the Upper Midwest's largest and most popular ethnic festivals. And fortunately for me, I had a front-row seat as I watched Paul deftly piece together all of his field notes and bits of research and then transform them into an engaging and insightful anthropological study.

Shortly before Paul's thesis defense and final examination (December 2006), I encouraged him to think about publishing his study as a book one day–so that others could benefit from his rich observations and intriguing discoveries. And now that day has come.

It is both a great honor and a real privilege for me to write these words of introduction to Paul's book about the Norsk Høstfest. Yet this is a study that is about much more than a single Scandinavian festival. In true holistic fashion, Paul convincingly demonstrates how this annual celebration is the focal point for the many powerful forces that have come to shape and define its special character–especially globalization, localization, and ethnicity. This study breaks new ground and thus represents a tremendous achievement. But good as it is, I believe this book is only the tip of the proverbial iceberg. Paul Emch is an individual with a multitude of talents and he has the potential to become one of our region's brightest and most innovative scholars. Truly, this book marks the beginning of even more and better things still to come.

Dr. Timothy J. Kloberdanz ("Tim")
Professor Emeritus
Department of Sociology & Anthropology
North Dakota State University

# Contents

# Abstract

This study focuses on Norwegian-American foodways and related food traditions that have been retained among Scandinavians who have lived in the Upper Midwestern United States for generations. It examines why certain foodways were maintained, whereas others were not, and what the overall significance of foodways is among Norwegian Americans. This study analyzes the prominent role that ethnic food plays in the context of Norwegian-American culture in the Upper Midwest through a holistic analysis of the Norsk Høstfest celebration. The festival is the largest Scandinavian-American folk event in North America and is held each October in Minot, North Dakota. In examining this festival, major emphasis has been placed on the impact that globalization has on Norwegian-American culture in the Upper Midwest. More specifically, it is the collision of the forces of globalization and localization within the Norsk Høstfest that are assessed. In the study of cultural dynamics, it is increasingly apparent that the examination of major events, such as the Norsk Høstfest, can be a particularly effective means for understanding the culture of the ethnic groups to which such events belong. Festivals are an excellent setting for the celebration and performance of cultural identity through the use of symbols. With a careful analysis of the Norsk Høstfest through use of the semiotic method, the intended meanings and messages of the festival can be ascertained. A close examination of these meanings and messages offers a profound glimpse into what it means to be Norwegian American.

# Introduction

"Events sometimes take on a life of their own and people's lives, their cultures, and the world are never again quite the same."

From Philip Carl Salzman's
*The Anthropology of Real Life* (1999:10)

## Interpreting Norwegian-American Foodways

This study is vital to bringing about an understanding of the cultural dynamics of North Dakota and also the Upper Midwest, where so many Norwegians have settled. Throughout the course of the research for this topic, I was amazed to find that there has been virtually no in-depth study of the Norsk Høstfest, which is held annually each October in Minot, North Dakota. This festival has grown to gigantic proportions, attracting upwards of sixty thousand people annually. A festival of this magnitude obviously must have some great significance to those directly involved in its planning and execution as well as to those who are solely attendees.

Some might view the Norsk Høstfest as little more than a celebration of sentimental ideals that holds little practical relevance for today. I argue, however, that this festival is, in fact, very relevant to contemporary issues, such as the maintenance of cultural identity in a rapidly changing world. More specifically, this study examines the collision of localized Norwegian-American culture with outside, globalized influences while, at the same time, analyzing the expression and perpetuation of ethnic identity through the use of foodways within the framework of the Norsk Høstfest celebration.

1

Analyzing the significance of this festival specifically through the realm of foodways has yielded excellent results. Because foodways are so thoroughly integrated into Norwegian-American culture and because of the great emotional significance that is often associated with them, this systematic analysis of foodways has proven to be quite revealing.

New ground has certainly been broken with this topic. Although it has been a difficult task—as there has not been an abundance of scholarly work done in this area—it has also presented an exciting challenge. To date, there has been no in-depth study in which the Norsk Høstfest is classified and examined in terms of being the comprehensive symbol of Norwegian-American culture that I assert it is. Fortunately, there is a modest collection of publications that deal with the symbolic nature of Norwegian-American foodways, which has helped to direct this aspect of the study. However, by and large much of this study is the product of original research.

It is widely accepted within the field of cultural anthropology that much can be learned about ethnic groups through the diligent analysis of their festivals and other cultural events (e.g., Geertz 1973, Magliocco 2006, and Salzman 1999). In this study, I have examined extensively the symbolic qualities of food. If food is to be classified as symbol, then it is vital to assess not only what it symbolizes, but most importantly, why it has come to be a symbol in the first place.

The Norsk Høstfest is an exceptionally meaningful event to those involved in it. Because of this, evaluating it in terms of symbolizing Norwegian-American culture has much merit. Although Norwegian-American culture is deep and thickly-encoded, I am confident that an approach that analyzes both foodways and the festival will yield a deeper understanding of Norwegian-American culture in the Upper Midwest.

# Methods

## Semiotic Analysis

Because foodways serve as such powerful symbols for group identity, the problems encountered while studying continuity and change are multifaceted and require application of the semiotic method as well as "thick description" as defined by one of America's foremost cultural anthropologists, Clifford Geertz. This will allow for the Norsk Høstfest to be condensed into more readily understandable terms.

Culture, as Geertz sees it, is inextricably linked with signification and symbol, and the examination of a particular group's symbols can reveal much about them. One of the most admirable qualities of Geertz is that he endeavors to answer the "why" question, rather than the "what" question (e.g., why people do the things they do). In so doing, he invariably delves into the very particular details of a culture in the quest for those things that particular group values as most significant.

> Once human behavior is seen as...symbolic action—action which, like phonation in speech, pigment in painting, line in writing, or sonance in music, signifies—the question as to whether culture is patterned conduct or a frame of mind, or even the two somehow mixed together, loses sense....The thing to ask is what their import is: what it is...in their occurrence and through their agency is getting said. (1973:10)

My research is largely based on the premise that people communicate much about themselves and their culture through shared cultural symbols

3

and through shared symbolic action. This symbolic action reveals itself in a variety of behaviors relating to foodways and food choice among Norwegian Americans. Festivals are an excellent setting for the performance of cultural identity through the use of these symbols, and I assert that food is quite possibly the most powerful symbol used within contemporary Norwegian-American culture to convey meaning. The Norsk Høstfest is an ideal venue for the assertion of Norwegian-American cultural identity because it seems to represent the epitome of Norwegian-American culture. Understanding the meanings expressed through foodways is a daunting task that requires meticulous study and paying keen attention to the details. Rather than solely seeking to identify characteristics of the culture to be interpreted, it is far more beneficial to assess why a people group is the way it is. According to Geertz:

> We must, in short, descend into detail, past the misleading tags, past the metaphysical types, past the empty similarities to grasp firmly the essential character of not only the various cultures but the various sorts of individuals within each culture, if we wish to encounter humanity face to face. (1973:53)

To embark on the task of understanding the symbolism and often deeply encoded messages within a culture that is not one's own can be a profoundly complex task. One can come to an understanding—if only a rudimentary understanding—of a given culture through paying close attention to details. Truly understanding a culture and all its complexities and particulars enables the anthropologist to be able to distinguish a wink from a twitch. In this sense, the "what" question is important, but the "why" question takes it one step further, digging ever deeper in the search for meaning. From a Geertzian perspective, God is very much in the details.

The semiotic approach to interpreting culture has been very useful to this study, because it hinges on the premise that culture exists to give life meaning. According to Dolgin et al., in *Symbolic Anthropology*, because symbolic approaches concentrate on meaning and the elements of signification (objects, persons, relations, and acts), understanding these processes of assigning meaning provides a window into understanding how people act within, interpret, and communicate about their world (1977:29).

## Participant Observation

The methodology of my fieldwork during my time at the Norsk Høstfest was primarily that of participant observation. I volunteered to work in the Scandinavian Kitchen on the last day of the festival in 2005, and for all four days during the 2006 festival (Figure 1). I gained many valuable insights and met some very interesting and helpful people.

Figure 1. The author serving food at the Scandinavian Kitchen (Photo by Krisanne Emch, October 15, 2005; Minot, ND).

The first day of my fieldwork at the Norsk Høstfest was the final day of the 2005 festival, so the festivities were in the process of drawing to a close. Two of my informants, Sven and Kjersti, told me that it had been by far more hectic the previous three days. On that particular day, the senior chefs had much more time to spend answering my questions. After having been there for awhile and becoming acclimated to the kitchen atmosphere, I began to wander around and talk to the various people there. It was very enlightening to get the views of individuals who are truly knowledgeable in the areas of traditional foodways.

In any event, my fieldwork at the Norsk Høstfest has provided an excellent working knowledge of the group and has provided the units of analysis with which to measure continuity and change. It has helped to address the most pressing issues—how the forces of localization and globalization affect Norwegian-American culture as a whole, as well as the nature of the festival itself, and how to decipher the metaphoric meanings encoded in the traditional Norwegian foodways displayed at this festival. The extensive use of semiotic analysis has been crucial in this endeavor.

I have interviewed many people of Norwegian-American heritage throughout North Dakota and the surrounding area, focusing on the main theme of what it means to be a Norwegian American. Of my thirty-three chief informants, eighteen were quoted directly within this text. The age range was quite broad, consisting of eight individuals in the twenty to thirty-year-old range, ten in the thirty-one to sixty-year-old range, and fifteen who were sixty-one and above. The ethnic background of the informants was mostly Scandinavian, and the individuals from the sixty-one and above group were all of Scandinavian background. There were various reasons why fifteen of these individuals were not quoted directly in this study. One reason was the repetition of many of the same themes and opinions among the informants. Another reason was that several of the informants were essentially unwilling or unable to elaborate as extensively as others. Finally, some of the informants simply expressed their thoughts more concisely, and so lent themselves more appropriately to being quoted.

It has been quite enlightening to study how this ties into and is reinforced through ethnic foodways. Many of the individuals interviewed have had substantial experience with the Norsk Høstfest. Also, several of the informants revealed information that I had never even considered, thereby enriching and broadening the scope of this project. These factors have had a great influence on the development of this study and have given it added weight. The vast majority of my interviews were tape recorded and transcribed, while a few were casual, non-recorded interviews.

One chief drawback with tape-recorded interviews is the laborious tran-scription process. For the most part though, I have found tape-recorded interviews to be by far the most advantageous method, as recording the interviews allows the interviewer to pay closer attention and thus get bet-ter details, rather than having to scramble to take notes.

The method of participant observation that has been so invaluable throughout this project has involved informal interviews, direct observa-tion, and participation. Participant observation has been indispensable to me, not only at the festival, but to a greater extent through my experienc-es with my various Norwegian American in-laws' many family gatherings, stories, and *lefse*-making events. This ethnographic method has proven very helpful because it is an excellent means of tapping into local points of view. It is an effective method by which to identify significant catego-ries of human experience more intimately. Participant observation is in-valuable for developing an insider's view of what is happening in a given situation. In the course of my preliminary fieldwork, I not only witnessed what was going on, but I also experienced, to a limited extent, what it was like to be a part of the group. The challenge is to combine participation and observation so as to become capable of understanding the experience as an insider, while also describing the experience for outsiders.

Since many of the senior chefs I talked to at the Høstfest were from Norway, many of my questions to them regarded the "authenticity" of the festival. One example of the type of questions I asked was, "How is the food in Norway different from the food served at Høstfest, and how authentic is it?" According to my chef-informants, the food was lacking in authenticity, as was the dress and some of the other cultural markers displayed at the festival. Another question that I addressed in my field-work at Høstfest related to the degree of commercialization of the festival. Kjersti, a chef from Stavanger, Norway, stated that Høstfest was just too big and commercialized, and that the authenticity of the food suffered as a result. The responses of my informants were not unexpected. It is important to keep in mind that the Norsk Høstfest is first and foremost a Norwegian-American festival representing a localized culture still cling-ing to its Norwegian roots, from which it has long been separated.

One important thing I considered was the effect of localization, as well as globalization, on the structure of the festival. The effects of localization are important, because the Norwegian-American immigrants who settled in the Upper Midwest represent a closed community, separated from their mother culture for at least a century. The result of this isolation is a very distinct and localized culture, which is based on the parent culture but is largely forged through the influence of local conditions and experiences.

I found that analyzing the effects of globalization is important because of the culturally diverse atmosphere and the international aspects displayed at the festival. These factors greatly influence the structuring of the festival, as it puts forth its own unique version of localized Norwegian-American culture tailored to the tastes of an increasingly globalized community.

The one thing that has become exceedingly clear about the question of authenticity in this study is that "authenticity" is a very relative concept—it all depends on who is being asked. What is authentic to Norwegian Americans in North Dakota may not be authentic to contemporary Norwegians from modern Norway.

In order to assess the many ways in which Norwegian-American cultural ideals are expressed, it has become apparent that a specific series of inquiries was needed. Such questions have arisen through much study and observation, and have, above all, emphasized the more pertinent focus—why these specific attitudes and inclinations exist in Norwegian-American culture.

# Content Questions

I have addressed a number of key questions throughout the course of the field research for this project. Below is a summary of some of the more pertinent questions that have emerged.

The five primary themes that were addressed are as follows:

- **The symbolic nature of foodways.**

Based on the work of Clifford Geertz, what is the role of symbols within Norwegian foodways, and how are these symbols integrated into the overall culture?

- **The role of foodways within the context of festival.**

Food is obviously an integral part of the Norsk Høstfest, as there is so much emphasis on the food vendors and ethnic cuisine featured at the festival.

- **The extent to which festival exists as a venue for the performance of culture.**

Performance is an essential aspect of human communicative capacity that depends on the use of semiotic behavior. Performance theory has played a very prominent role in this study.

- **The function of foodways as a bridge between local and global culture, as well as the past and the present.**

Anthropologists Linda Keller Brown and Kay Mussell state that shared foodways have a unifying ability so symbolically powerful that they can unite members of the group separated geographically, and possibly even those separated by death (1984:13). Thus, foodways seem to be the perfect medium for connecting people and bridging differences.

- **Religious Traditions.**

Norwegian immigrants who came to America were predominantly Lutherans, and many of their descendants still are. Thus, what is the role of religion in contemporary Norwegian-American foodways and culture? The list of specific questions as they were presented to the informants is as follows:

1. How do you think food is used to symbolize or represent Norwegian-American culture? For example, is food more than just food among Norwegian- Americans?

2. What part does ethnic food play in the grand picture of the Norsk Høstfest?

3. How is the Norsk Høstfest a means of promoting and demonstrating Norwegian-American culture?

4. In what ways do you think the Norsk Høstfest helps to link local and perhaps international audiences?

5. In what ways does the Norsk Høstfest link traditions of the past and the present?

6. To what extent do you think the Norsk Høstfest might be a celebration of being Norwegian or Lutheran?

7. In your opinion, are Norwegian-American foodways tied in with any religious beliefs? Can you give any examples?

8. What are the characteristics of a good Norwegian?

This list of questions has proven to be quite helpful and has been a true asset to this study. These questions have been tailored and condensed considerably from the initial list of fourteen overly complex questions with which I started. It has taken considerable work to get these questions into shape, and it has been a continual process throughout this study. Some of the initial interviews undertaken in the early portions of this study also helped to uncover new ways of further tailoring these questions in order to make them more "inform-ant friendly."

To be sure, the final question (i.e., what are the characteristics of a good Norwegian?) has proven at times to be both the most difficult as well as the most productive. The reason that this was a somewhat dif-ficult question is that it is quite direct, and perhaps even a little blunt. It sometimes took people by surprise, and often produced a few moments of silent contemplation. It seemed to make most informants earnestly analyze what they would personally define as the best characteristics of Norwegian Americans. Though this question was somewhat difficult at first, after most of the informants were given the chance to think about it for a while, it produced some concise and even revelatory assessments.

These questions have provided a structured framework to guide the interviews. Sometimes I would ask these questions in sequence, and other times not. I have found that in many cases it was quite advanta-geous to simply let the informants talk, and once they had touched on a theme of one of the questions, I would then formally pose that question for them. This technique has yielded excellent results, because in a way it helped not only to better prepare the informants for the question but also to enable them to answer the question more adequately in their own words. Employing these questions has certainly helped get to the heart of Norwegian-American cultural identity—by examining the processes by which the ethnic and regional traditions of Norwegian-American culture are incorporated with the new trends of an increasingly globalized world.

# Theory

## Globalization

Globalization is a fascinating process in which the nature of cultures and the ways that they interact with one another are constantly changing. Globalization is the primary theory utilized in this study, and it has proven quite applicable in numerous ways. Though globalization is the major theory applied in this case, a consistent undercurrent of Geertzian interpretive theory is at work throughout the study as well. Globalization has been united with interpretive theory, and essentially Geertz is supplemented with globalization theory.

According to anthropologist and ethnographer Sabina Magliocco, the parameters of globalization are multifaceted and include the expansion of free market capitalism, the internationalization of business, the spread of global politics, the expansion of international relations, and the mass movements of peoples across national boundaries (2006:xii). In particular, what we are talking about is the emergence of what social-cultural anthropologist Arjun Appadurai calls a "world society" beyond the nation state, transcending old divisions such as urban/rural and center/periphery, cultural homogenization, and the emergence of postcolonial cultures (1990:296–299).

Magliocco describes globalization as often being construed as the growing Westernization or Americanization of world cultures (2006:xii). However, this standpoint can be problematic since it implies a one-way movement of culture, as Appadurai says, "from the West to the rest," ignoring cultural flows that can move in many directions (1990:295). The

11

issue we are addressing in this present case is the progressive alteration
of ethnic culture in the Upper Midwest toward a trend of globalization.

The "Americanization" of which Magliocco speaks appears to be very
much a factor here in the Midwest as well. As a result of this Americanization
of groups in America to what can be viewed as a more mainstream culture, many aspects of the traditional lifestyles are no longer practiced.
In the context of the festival, however, tradition and cultural ideals not
only have survived the forces of social transformation, but also manage to
thrive in this new environment. Recent scholarship has served to bolster
this theory. Anthropologist Clara Gallini, who has done extensive work
regarding festive events, notes with regard to Sardinian festival, "In these
last years the [festival] has been the object of very showy forms of revival....The *festa* is triumphantly entering into the consumer economy"
(1971:12). Furthermore, anthropologist F. E. Manning, with regard to festival and cultural performance, states that "throughout both industrialized
and developing nations, new celebrations are being created and older ones
revived on a scale...unmatched in human history" (1983:4).

The Norsk Høstfest is by no means exempt from this phenomenon that
Gallini and Manning have documented. The Høstfest is very showy in
nature, and constitutes a rich display of the most treasured—albeit no
longer commonplace—aspects of Norwegian-American culture. For example, it is fairly certain that most Norwegian-American families no longer
eat *lutefisk, lefse,* or *rømmegrøt* on a daily basis. Many, in fact, partake of
these and other ethnic delicacies only in the context of certain holidays or
the Norsk Høstfest. In this way, the festival is not so much a celebration of
contemporary Norwegian-American culture, but rather that of a bygone
era—a "golden age" of Norwegian-American culture, so to speak.

Although the Høstfest does showcase specific cultural attributes that
can seem quite anachronistic at times, it is at the same time on the cutting
edge of the global scene. The organizers of the Norsk Høstfest are well
aware of the fact that in order for the festival to remain vital and successful, it needs to reach out beyond Minot. A great example of this is found
in the food that is available at Høstfest today. Church basement foods
such as *lutefisk, lefse,* and homemade meatballs are classic Norwegian-
American fare, but before long people want more variety. Perhaps that is
why trained, professional chefs from all over Scandinavia are brought in
each year. The foods available at Høstfest constitute a rich blend of tastes
from the past and present. The classic, highly traditional Norwegian-
American foods that are relished by many are great cultural symbols and
always will have a special place at the Norsk Høstfest. However, people
also want to experience the foods that modern Scandinavians enjoy. In

this way, the Norsk Høstfest does a great job of blending elements of the past and present, the local and the global.

Globalization and the socioeconomic changes that it can often bring with it are more often than not reflected in a community's festivals. The importance given to festivals will often change in response to economic change. Moreover, Magliocco asserts that the changes imposed on festivals by the forces of globalization and modernization are not limited to the financial or structural aspects, but rather the symbolic nature of the festival itself:

> Festivals are constantly evolving in response to current conditions. Festive change is brought about by individuals who, acting singly or together as arbiters of their own symbolic systems, initiate meaningful changes to bring the festivals more in concert with the new situation. (2006:129)

According to Magliocco, the entry of festivals into the consumer economy has caused a number of changes in festival structure relating to the very function and meaning of the festival. The same elements that have allowed festivals to become vehicles for consumer products also make them an excellent means for the playing out of social conflicts, both large and small. In many ways, festival is grounded in two worlds, that of the macro-world of the consumer economy and the micro-world of local concerns. In the same way, those who organize them are often influenced by both worlds and strive to use the available cultural materials to make a statement through the festival (2006:3).

There is no doubt that the world is certainly getting smaller. Though the Midwest is very much integrated into the rest of the world, it still maintains its own distinct regional characteristics. A curious tendency exists in America, and especially in the Upper Midwest, to view the persistence of ethnic identity as somehow "un-American." What we see within Norwegian-American culture is a quiet defiance of the mainstream—up until the Norsk Høstfest. Once within the context of this festival, however, all the cherished traditions are openly showcased without fear of negative judgments from others. Folk festivals such as the Norsk Høstfest exist in part to assert the unique ethnic and regional traditions that are still valued and practiced in the Midwest, while at the same time acknowledging the larger global community and their place within it.

I assert that attending and participating in the Norsk Høstfest is, in a sense, a nostalgic revival of cultural heritage, and a kind of sentimental education for those of Norwegian-American background. This is true because the Norsk Høstfest is a text, in that it is an integrated cultural document that clearly lays out the parameters of Norwegian-American culture for all who care to take note. To call on a Geertzian theme in this case, it can be said that the themes and meanings of the Høstfest are largely communicated through a "vocabulary of sentiment" that pervades to the very core of Norwegian-American cultural identity (1973:449).

Perhaps it is this sentimental nature of Norwegian-American culture that makes an ethnographic interpretation of it so challenging. It is true that most cultures do not readily give up their secrets, nor yield themselves to interpretations, if sincere and concerted ethnographic efforts are not made to study them. Norwegian-American culture is deep and full of meaning, and the Norsk Høstfest exists as one principal text that helps in understanding it. As Geertz has asserted, "The culture of a people is an ensemble of texts, themselves ensembles, which the anthropologist strains to read over the shoulders of those to whom they properly belong" (1973:452).

## Localization of Culture

Localization, like globalization, is a very important concept within the framework of this festival. The dynamics of the Norsk Høstfest cannot be fully appreciated without a working understanding of the concept of localization. Localization can be defined as the adaptation of a given culture to its particular environment over time. This adaptation is what makes culture the distinct and ever-changing phenomenon that it is. Many Norwegian Americans still feel a certain degree of connection to the old homeland and enjoy celebrating their heritage. Due to geographic and cultural isolation, however, Norwegian and Norwegian-American cultures have taken divergent paths. Because of this, the broad effects of localization are quite evident.

Within the framework of the Norsk Høstfest, three very distinct cultural identities find expression. The Norsk Høstfest is, in fact, a celebration of the interactions of these three identities.

The first cultural identity is that of contemporary Norway. Norway today is a highly modernized and industrialized nation. Far from the destitute, overpopulated place that it once was during the era of emigration in the nineteenth century, it is now a land of plenty.

Second is the current Norwegian-American cultural identity found in the Upper Midwestern United States today. This group, made up of mostly third and fourth-generation Norwegian immigrants, represents a transplanted Norwegian culture that has developed to a great extent independently from its parent nation. This group is highly integrated into mainstream Midwestern culture but still preserves many cherished traditions of its proud Norwegian heritage.

Finally, there is the Norwegian-American culture as it developed in the early days of settlement in America. This cultural identity differs markedly from either of the previous two. It is a commemoration of the union of Norwegian and American cultures during the era of immigration a century or more ago. It is this third rendering of Norwegian culture that is displayed and celebrated especially in the context of the Norsk Høstfest. It represents a hybridized culture that upholds and showcases the "best" attributes of both cultures. It tends to focus on those classical themes of Norwegian cultural history with which individuals most prefer to identify. Inevitably, those things that bring about warm recollections and a sense of pride will be most prevalent and are, therefore, most likely to be displayed as markers for cultural solidarity.

It should be noted that, to date, this third phenomenon has had the most profound impact on shaping Norwegian-American cultural identity today. Contemporary Norwegian-American culture in the Upper Midwest, as it is displayed at the Norsk Høstfest in particular, is a revival and a celebration of what life was like in those early days, after immigration to America. These cherished cultural themes find expression in a number of ways: festive dress, arts and crafts, use of the Norwegian language, and especially traditional foodways. For an example of how localization and foodways come into play within the Norwegian-American culture displayed at the Høstfest, we need only to examine *lutefisk* and *lefse*. According to Lori and Jim Olson, these foods have become symbolic traditions among Norwegian Americans, in part because they are the same foods that helped their ancestors survive the migration west after arriving in America a century ago. It is only natural that these foods that were so important to the settlers would have such a prominent place within Norwegian-American culture and would become a centerpiece of the Norsk Høstfest whose theme is the preservation of this heritage (1995:48).

So, through the celebration of this highly localized rendition of Norwegian-American culture, the cherished traditions are remembered, celebrated, and preserved. But the Høstfest also serves another very important purpose. Simply put, the Norsk Høstfest serves as an environment where issues of globalization and localization can safely be addressed and integrated. Globalization is a vital force, which affords the Midwest a connection to the rest of the world. In the context of this festival, globalization exists not to replace or undermine localized cultural norms, but rather to acknowledge their value and uphold them while at the same time acting as a balancing force by bringing in vital outside influences. Given the highly localized nature of the Norsk Høstfest, in the sense that it is largely tailored to the expectations and standards of local Norwegian-American culture, it does function extremely well as a symbol of Norwegian-American culture in the Upper Midwest. Because this feature of the Høstfest is well-established, it creates a safe environment where issues surrounding the change brought about by way of globalization can be addressed.

The prospect of change can be a source of anxiety for many people, and this is certainly true of people in the Upper Midwest. This anxiety may not be vocalized or explicitly observable, but it certainly exists on the subconscious level. People in general seem to prefer change to come in small doses, spread out over long periods of time. Change is almost never easy, but it is a necessary and fundamental part of a viable culture. The Upper Midwest is no longer isolated from the rest of the world and has not been for quite some time. Within the perspective of the Norsk Høstfest, it is acknowledged that though much has changed, and more change is yet to come, many of the old ways will still live on and be maintained through the festival. These time-honored traditions and values are maintained in this case, largely through the use of foodways, simply because food can serve both as a binding force as well as a system for asserting cultural distinctiveness within Norwegian-American culture.

# Literature Review

Foodways are often laden with emotion and significance for both old and new Americans alike, because food can serve as such a strong symbol of ethnic identity. According to Linda Keller Brown and Kay Mussell, recent scholarship within anthropology has served to change our perceptions of culture from that of "thingness" to that of "process" (1984:44). Anthropologists are not so much concerned with defining ethnicity as a category with certain measurable characteristics and traits, but as a cultural and social process in which the relationships of individuals and groups and the communication of identity are most significant. Social relationships are developed and maintained by symbols, and the symbols are often how others perceive a group. In this way, foodways can actually come to symbolize the group itself.

Fredrik Barth, a Norwegian anthropologist and ethnographer, has written that ethnic groups are a form of social organization for which the significant characteristic is self ascription or ascription by others in the group:

> A categorical ascription is an ethnic ascription when it classifies a person in terms of his basic, most general identity, presumptively determined by his origin and background. To the extent that actors use ethnic identities to categorize themselves and others for purposes of interaction, they form ethnic groups in this organizational sense. (1969:13)

Barth states that in order for ethnic identity to be preserved, ethnic groups must maintain boundaries between their group and others. The cultural themes and features used to signify these boundaries may differ

17

from group to group and may change over time, but ultimately the boundaries are maintained. But in order for ethnic groups to thrive and maintain
their distinct cultural heritage in the midst of other differing cultures, they
not only need "signals for identification, but also a structuring of interaction which allows for the persistence of cultural differences" (1969:16).
According to Barth, these guidelines are what mold intergroup relations.

The fundamental tenets of the symbolism found in foodways can be
broken down into four interrelated categories of food symbolism. The first
of these, according to Carole Counihan, an anthropologist who focuses on
food studies and gender, is that specific meanings and symbols can be encoded in individual food items within specific contexts (1999:20). What
French literary critic, social theorist, and semiotician Roland Barthes describes as "food's symbolic malleability" allows it to be an effective medium for accommodating diverse cultural ideologies (1997:57).

In essence, different cultures can endow foods with arbitrary meanings. These meanings manifest themselves not only in the way a food is
perceived in terms of its color, taste, texture, and smell, but also in the
preparation methods, manner, and order in which it is served (Counihan
1999:114). Paul Fieldhouse, in his work on food and culture, states that
food may be invested with meanings of prestige and power, such as
Trobriand Island yams and Western caviar. Food can also confer status
and sociability, as in the Native American potlatch, or it can mirror gender and sexuality ideals, such as the sacred cow as a symbol of fertility in
India (1986:175).

Food can signify protest and dissention, such as the refusal to eat
McDonald's Big Macs or Coca-Cola as a means to "rebel" against the
"evils" of globalization. Cultural events are often defined by the foods con-
sumed, such as wedding cakes at a reception or turkey at Thanksgiving.
Symbolic food anthropologist Simon R. Charsley writes that foods can
embody meaning simply by their linguistic association, such as in Chinese
culture, where noodles represent long life, or they may symbolize normative cultural values, such as chicken noodle soup as "comfort food." There
are diverse ways in which food is granted the capacity to symbolize, and
while individualized food symbols are not only culturally dependent and
fluid, they are also interpreted on a macro and micro basis (1992:3).

However, as Charsley points out, these individualized meanings are essentially insignificant because, like any symbol, food acquires meaning
within the context of a given symbolic system (1992:3). For example, if
Western culture did not consider such foods as caviar to be symbols of
prosperity and wealth, then their consumption by individuals would not
in any way signify a person's cultural knowledge of the "fine" things in

life, nor would it showcase an individual's wealth in being able to afford such delicacies. The same situation can apply to the Thanksgiving turkey. If a given culture considers sausage as "the" ideal Thanksgiving meal, then the turkey as a food item is insignificant to the "sausage culture." Ultimately, context is everything within a particular culture, especially when it comes to ideals and beliefs about what is the most important determinant of a food's meaning.

The foods of certain cultural groups can also denote inclusion and exclusion of individuals based on cultural, moral, gender, or religious grounds. According to sociologist and social anthropologist Anne Murcott, because eating and drinking are ultimately cultural affairs, a sense of community and belonging can be fostered and confirmed based on one's adherence or lack thereof to a set of food rules (1986:108). As Charsley states:

> The inclusionary and exclusionary aspect of food reinforces symbolic boundaries by recognizing and reaffirming a group's distinctiveness through the medium of food commonality. Through enculturation, individuals learn which foods to eat, which to abstain from, what foods constitute a cultural meal and when to eat. These preferences reinforce culture, while excluding all those who fail to conform to these culinary patterns. (1992:3)

Some examples of this are that Muslims know other Muslims and Jews know other Jews by their shared participation in fasting during Ramadan and eating kosher foods, respectively. In the same way, one good "Norskie" may know another good "Norskie" at Høstfest by their mutual appreciation for *lutefisk*.

Mary Douglas, the well-known British anthropologist who has written extensively on the role of symbols in human culture, has popularized a second area of food symbolism—the notion that food is socially meaningful to groups, whether it is meals, feasts, categories of foods, or groups of foods. According to Douglas, food categories and groups encode social events because the groupings of foods are an inevitable byproduct and reflection of the rules and structure of a society's organization on both broad and intimate levels (1972). To further emphasize this point, Douglas goes on to state:

> Because foods and groups of foods are structurally reflective of social rules, conditions, taboos and boundaries and because they implicate the symbolic and material conditions of society, the examination of such food groups can reveal concepts of hierarchy, inclusion and exclusion, symbolic boundaries and social relations. (1972:61)

According to symbolic anthropologist and behavioral scientist Leslie Gofton, Douglas's concepts of hierarchy imply issues of power and class in relationship to an individual's position (i.e., the social and cultural food hierarchy). Food consumption, as with the cultural consumption of resources, can be a vehicle for social differentiation, an embodiment of class inequality and the stratification of knowledge, as well as aesthetic sensibility and values (1986:141). Gofton goes on to say that knowing which cutlery to use for which dish or the appropriateness of certain foods at certain meals can be an indicator of one's position within the social hierarchy. But hierarchy is not merely encoded by one's knowledge of food, but also by one's cultural understanding of and preferences for food (1986:142).

From this explanation, we can see that certain foods are perceived to be more privileged than others—banquet foods over fast foods, caviars over sour cream. It then follows that those who have access to these symbolically privileged foods are conferred the social position that these foods represent. According to Gofton, a good example of this can be observed in looking at how food rationing in Napoleon's army was organized. In Napoleon's army, the officers ate lobster while the lowly soldiers ate salt pork, thus typifying French societal hierarchy during the time period (1986:142).

A third direction that symbolic food anthropology has embarked on, according to Appadurai, is that meanings can be seen in the oral and written traditions of cooking, namely oral stories and recipes about food and cookbooks (1986:36). Not only do oral and written traditions reflect changing attitudes about what is edible (i.e., they serve as a gauge as to what is socially acceptable), they also signify the greater culture from which those traditions emerged. These oral and written food recollections are a part of cultural history. Along this stream of thought, food does not simply symbolize an idea or part of culture, nor does it represent the structure of culture; food is a representation of culture itself. When individuals share their oral traditions or read of others' cooking habits, food semantics, or the meanings of foods in different civilizations, the image of "foreign" cultures can be discerned. Why is *bannock* important in some Native American cultures? Why are there myths surrounding corn in Mexican society and moon cake in Chinese society? These oral traditions are simply a part of the culture.

The final approach within symbolic food anthropology that will be expounded is that meanings can be attached to culturally shared food events. According to Fieldhouse, the food "culture" subscribed to by a given group represents a collection of learned attitudes and behaviors that dictate not only what is acceptable as food, but also when and how that food is to be prepared, served, and eaten (1986:48). Because dominant values of a given culture influence all aspects of food-related activity, it becomes vital to instill in individuals the social, cultural, and psychological values of food and food events.

As British anthropologist Jack Goody has asserted, all of the idiosyncrasies that emerge from commonly shared food rituals, such as foods chosen, methods of eating and preparation, utensils utilized, and time of eating, are a part of an integrated cultural pattern in which custom and practice have a part to play (1982:13).

## Performance and Symbols

These theories can help us to see how effectively symbols are used within a culture to signify group identity. Barth (1969) focuses on the "performance" of identity through the manipulation of shared cultural symbols. These symbols of identification function as a playbook of sorts, which guides the course of events within group interaction. Since cultural symbols serve this vital function, application of this theory of culture as a "performance" is essential within the context of the Norsk Høstfest, which is lauded as North America's largest Scandinavian festival.

Fredrik Barth urges taking into account what the actors themselves consider most significant, since "some cultural features are used by the actors as signals and emblems of differences; others are ignored" (1969:14). According to Barth, the cultural signals displayed by the actors are of two types: first, "overt signals or signs—the diacritical features that people look for and exhibit to show identity, often such features as dress, language, house-form, or general style of life; second, "basic value orientations: the standards of morality and excellence by which performance is judged."

Another anthropologist, Abner Cohen, defines the central theoretical problem of cultural anthropology as the "dialectical relations between symbolic action and power relationships," and offers us further insights into the processes of ethnicity and performance (1944:13–14). Cohen defines the kinds of symbols he is discussing as:

> Objects, acts, concepts, or linguistic formations that stand ambiguously for a multiplicity of disparate meanings, evoke sentiments and emotions, and impel men to action. They usually occur in stylized patterns of activities like ceremonial, ritual, gift exchange, prescribed forms of joking, taking an oath, eating and drinking together. (1944:v)

Symbols like those listed by Cohen serve to help individuals develop a sense of self and to confront human problems, such as life and death.

Thus, they are both expressive and instrumental. The symbol system is flexible in that symbols can be replaced, different symbols can perform the same function, and the same symbol can change its function. What looks like a continuity of symbols may, upon closer analysis, reveal old forms being used to meet new needs (1944).

One of the most important functions for such symbols is the objectification of relationships between individuals and groups. Social relationships are developed and maintained by symbols, thus we tend to see groups through their symbols and to identify ourselves through symbols. To Cohen, "All social behavior is couched in symbolic forms" and "symbolic behavior is dramatic behavior" (1944:30–34, 52).

## The Symbolism of Food and its Effects on Group Identity

Foodways are often laden with emotion and significance for both old and new Americans because food can serve as such a strong symbol of ethnic identity. The field of anthropology has begun more and more to view culture not as a concrete thing but rather as a constantly evolving entity. Anthropologists are not so much concerned with defining ethnicity as a category whose characteristics and traits we want to list, but as a social process in which the relationship of individuals and groups and the communication of identity are significant.

Social relationships are developed and maintained by symbols, and the symbols are how we perceive a group. In this way, foodways can actually come to symbolize the group itself. Fieldhouse goes into great detail as to how food, and particularly food use, is such an effective tool in the interpretation of diverse cultures:

> Truly, food usages are signposts to understanding different cultures. Patterns of food preparation, distribution and consumption reflect the dominant type of social relationships in a society. They are an expression of status and social distance, of political power and of family bonds. Food is extensively used in social intercourse as a means of expressing friendship and respect. The quality and quantity of food offered or shared reflects a common understanding of the closeness of various types of social relationships. Food is also used as a manipulative tool to purchase favors or to bring about desired behaviors, and as a weapon with which to humiliate rivals. It confers status through ownership or usage, and is commonly a part of ritual proceedings. Food is an indispensable element in festivals and celebrations where it may

be again symbolic of social relationships or where it may assume supernatural powers. (1986:105)

Symbolic food anthropology has been vital in redirecting anthropology towards addressing issues of culture and interpretation rather than grand macro-theories. The challenge, then, is to attempt to understand how and why people invest meaning into particular symbols and employ those symbols in everyday life.

## Foodways and the Symbolic Anthropology Perspective

The development of symbolic food theories has reflected a growing dissatisfaction with the direction of anthropological approaches during the second half of the twentieth century. During this "atheoretical" period, academics conceptualized food from an empirical, pseudo-scientific orientation (the Biological Paradigm). Food was discussed primarily in terms of its nutritious value (fats, sugars, and mineral composition) or vis-à-vis its evolutionary development (the Archaeological Paradigm, where and for whom the foodstuff was domesticated). In reaction to these static conceptions, anthropologists have turned to symbolic anthropology as a means of expanding the food concept in order to understand how food and culture are intimately related.

According to Dolgin et al., from the standpoint of symbolic anthropology, culture is composed of a system of symbols and assigned meanings shared within a common group of people (1977). Symbolic anthropologist Mary Des Chene states that the major focus of symbolic anthropology is studying the ways in which people understand and interpret their surroundings. These interpretations form a "shared cultural system of meaning, among members of the same society" (1996:1274). Dolgin et al. go on to state that because symbolic approaches concentrate on meaning and the elements of meaning (objects, persons, relations, and acts), understanding these processes of assigning meaning provides a window into understanding how people act within, interpret, and communicate about their world (1977). Des Chene asserts that this process of assigning meanings to symbols is dependent on a culturally specific symbolic code. This symbolic code is based on a shared cultural system of meaning that influences the social-organizational processes of a culture, as well as that culture's formulated reality (1996).

According to Des Chene, there are two major premises governing symbolic anthropology. The first is that "beliefs, however unintelligible, become comprehensible when understood as part of a cultural system of meaning" (1996:1274). The second major premise is that actions are guided by interpretation, allowing symbolism to aid in interpreting both ideal and material activities (Ibid).

In applying symbolic anthropology, culture can be understood by deciphering key symbols and rituals within the culture. Counihan states that food anthropologists believe that a society's culture can be understood by examining such key symbols as food, consumption habits, etc. Since eating is an essential activity and foodways constitute an organized system with its own food language, food can be construed as a prime realm for conveying meaning (1999). Marshall Sahlins, the renowned symbolic food anthropologist, asserts that by interpreting key symbols, food anthropologists can render seemingly unintelligible foodstuffs meaningful by contextualizing food within a socially patterned cultural structure (1990:95). Finally, Gofton states that "as a multi-leveled, multivocal symbol, food symbolizes themes, concepts, ideas and situations and signifies ways of life" (1986:145). By applying symbolic anthropology, the ethnographer is provided with the opportunity to study how the role of such symbols as food, religion, or even mythology guide and direct the everyday lives of individuals.

## Food and Religion

As already discussed, Norwegian immigrants who came to America were predominantly Lutheran, as many of their descendants still are. Obviously, the role religion plays in contemporary Norwegian-American foodways and culture must be an important one. Further analysis of this aspect has indicated that religion does indeed have a profound influence on Norwegian-American food culture.

Janet Letnes Martin and Suzanne Nelson, who coauthor a number of books on Norwegian-American foodways and culture, point out that one very common way that food and religion are tied together is the integration of food into the Lutheran church service experience. In their list entitled "Twenty Statements that Lutheran Women Can't Say, But at the Wrong Time of the Month, Might Think (Not Christian)," number twenty succinctly sums up the general feeling of Lutheran Church Basement Women regarding their unofficial church duties. "Why," they inquire, "do Lutherans think they have to eat every time they go to church?" (1994:111). It appears that many Lutheran Norwegian Americans equate the churchgoing experience with being fed. Obviously then, food plays a very significant role within the Norwegian-American Lutheran identity.

Letnes Martin and Nelson go into further detail about some of the possible symbolism of an all-time Norwegian-American favorite, cream peas on toast:

> ...the Cream Peas almost took on a Spiritual Aura. It was White like Purity and *Sankta Lucia* Gowns and Confirmation Robes. It was green like the Trinity Stoles and the Holy, Holy, Holy Altar Cloth. (1994:9)

In addition, The Lutheran Church Basement *Lutefisk* Supper seems to represent far more than just a good, hearty church meal, or even a reason to get together. The annual *Lutefisk* Supper was the Scandinavian version of the biblical miracle of the loaves and fishes, when Jesus fed the five-thousand. Consequently, say Letnes Martin and Nelson, the *Lutefisk* Supper moved into the realm of the sacred and became a consecrated event in a quasi-doctrinal sort of way:

> And it came to pass that the annual Church Basement *Lutefisk* Supper was kind of a holy day for Scandinavian Lutherans. It was a day of great anticipation and much preparedness, whether you came to eat or came to serve. It was a day when everyone in the church cleaned up, showed up, and sat together to partake in a meal of Scandinavian Holy Food. (1997:160)

Letnes Martin and Nelson go into great detail as to how the annual Church Basement *Lutefisk* Supper was conducted. The preparation and commencement of the dinner was undertaken in a very sanctified and methodical manner. The reader will notice the many references to "whiteness" and "purity" with regard to the food and decorations:

> Everything was done in an orderly hushed fashion. There was no pushing or shoving. There were no food fights. Everything about it seemed white and pure. The tables were covered and draped in white tablecloths. White snow that clung to Lutheran overshoes was stomped off unto the linoleum floor. White dishtowels were slung over the shoulders of the sweaty kitchen workers.

> Large, no nonsense, blonde Lutheran ladies mashed kettle after kettle of white potatoes and white rutabagas without complaining. Smaller and older white-haired Lutheran ladies with noticeable dowager's humps sat on stools in the kitchen arranging plates of off-white *lefse* and white Scandinavian goodies such as *krumkaker, berlinerkranser, fattigmann,* rosettes, spritz, and white sugar cookies. Those who were a little straighter but not strong enough to mash, stirred the creamy white *rømmegrøt* and poured it into small sauce dishes.

> The translucent, white, jellylike *lutefisk*, encased in white cheese cloth, was carefully lifted out of the boiling water. It looked like white-gauzed Sunday School angels. Immediately it was heaped unto white platters and was brought to the tables along with the rest of the food (1997:161–162).

These passages are absolutely loaded with symbolism. From them, one can clearly ascertain the high degree to which the Norwegian-American maxim of "white on white" comes into play. The Church Basement *Lutefisk* Supper would seem to be the epitome of the high degree of influence that religion brings to bear on foodways in Norwegian-American culture.

## Eating as a Social Experience

The task of delineating what is eaten is a complex one, but it is nothing compared to addressing the daunting question of why it is eaten. Food has always been much more than a source of nourishment; it plays a vital role in the social life, both religious and secular, of culture groups. The following list, which draws on the work of Bass, Wakefield, and Kolassa (1979), indicates some of the diverse uses of foods in society and includes both biological and cultural functions. Food can be used to

1. Satisfy hunger and nourish the body
2. Initiate and maintain personal and business relationships
3. Demonstrate the nature and extent of relationships
4. Provide a focus for communal activities
5. Express love and caring
6. Express individuality
7. Proclaim the separateness of a group
8. Demonstrate belongingness to a group
9. Cope with psychological or emotional stress
10. Reward or punish
11. Signify social status
12. Bolster self-esteem and gain recognition
13. Wield political and economic power
14. Prevent, diagnose, and treat physical illness
15. Prevent, diagnose, and treat psychological illness
16. Symbolize emotional experiences
17. Display piety
18. Represent security
19. Express moral sentiments
20. Signify wealth

Even a cursory glance through anthropological and sociological literature is enough to help us recognize that one's culture is a major determinant of what is eaten. While it is easily observed that the direct consequences of food intake are biological, with food meeting the energy and nutrient needs of the body, it is also apparent that the nature of food intake is shaped by social, religious, economic, and political processes. Nutritional anthropologist Diva Sanjur succinctly summarizes this idea by stating that "...food habits come into being and are maintained because they are effective, practical, and meaningful behaviors in a particular culture" (1982:18).

Jackie, a college student who had also spent some time doing research at the Høstfest for a paper, offered some interesting insights as to how food is used to represent Norwegian-American culture at the Norsk Høstfest:

> Maybe because it's a way for them to keep their everyday traditions from their home countries alive there. I know I was sitting down in the cafeteria area and I heard a guy, who was eating *lutefisk*, and he was like "Ooo, this is so good; this is just like how my mom used to make it." And I remember walking in there and hearing a lady say "smell that *sauerkraut!*" and I was just like hmm, okay. But it's just like, to them it's their soul food, and I think it reminds them of being young and their parents and I don't know, even if they haven't been in Germany or Norway or wherever, I think it just reminds them of their past. Food has a way of doing that, I suppose. Yeah, it [food] is a huge draw. I know there are tons of people who go just for the food, and, like, there are huge halls just filled and filled and filled with all these different types of food, and it's probably one of the main draws of the festival (Interview conducted on March 23, 2006; Fargo, ND).

The act of eating can certainly be a highly significant social experience, in that people can share a wealth of knowledge about themselves just through their food usage. Lester, a middle-aged informant, put it concisely in his personal analysis of the role food plays within social interaction:

> ...It seems like food in general is a way of inviting you in, I mean, it's a way of inviting people into your world....It allows you to share something of your past...to share some of the traditions of the food. I'm not sure I fully understand why that is, but it's a way of sharing something of you, as an individual. Who you are, your past...I'm sure that you think it tastes good, but it also brings memories that you want new people to interact with...

> And it's probably a way to share yourself, without talking about
> yourself, you know...it can be that—and acceptable. So instead
> of just sitting down with a stranger and talking about who I am,
> and what my past is, I can do that with food....You can share it
> as tangible, but yet it doesn't have to be too personal (Interview
> conducted on April 29, 2006; Grand Forks, ND).

It is certainly true that food allows people to speak volumes about themselves without uttering a single word. This quality of food proves especially
useful within the somewhat stoic, reserved Norwegian-American culture,
in which talking about one's self directly is often considered taboo.

Fieldhouse, citing N. W. Jerome (1969), says that people do communicate
who they are through their uses of food. He goes on to state that basic cultural
themes expressed in the U.S. are those of "individualism, democracy, capitalism, pluralism, industrialism, leisure and youthfulness" (1986:44).

While it is true that food and the act of eating have innumerable non-
biological uses and meanings, nowhere is this more evident than in the
everyday experiences of social interaction. Food is a vehicle for expressing group membership, for smoothing social interaction, and communicating friendship and acceptance. As Lester states:

> I remember Grandma Josephine. There's a pride about...people
> liking what you like, and Jack, her grandson, liked *rømmegrøt*
> and that was always a favorite thing, cause she would tell the sto-
> ry about whenever Jack was asked what was his favorite food, he
> would respond, "It's *rømmegrøt.*" I don't know how many times
> I've heard that story from Grandma. There was a sense of pride
> that one of her grandsons liked that....I think when people like
> something you like, it does produce a connection, you know. And
> that again gets to the food or to the social event to the sport...
> it's a point of connection (Interview conducted April 29, 2006;
> Grand Forks, ND).

Food use also abounds with status symbolism and is manipulated to
demonstrate differences in social standing, either subtly or blatantly. One
could apply a proverb to this phenomenon that would say, "Wherever two
or more are gathered, let there be food and drink in the midst of them."
According to Cohen, even those transitional life-cycle crises, such as the
rites of passage, are in almost all societies marked by the ritual or ceremo-
nial distribution and consumption of food (1944:13–14).

Culture, by its very nature and definition, is well integrated into the
lives of its bearers. Consequently, the profound part it plays in shaping
society is often taken for granted. This is especially true of food, which
can seem such an everyday part of life.

# Subconscious Culture

On the whole, we are unaware of much of our culture and are often completely oblivious to the rules that are in place to govern many aspects of our thought and behavior. Culture is internalized so that most of our routine behaviors are done unthinkingly, simply because "that's the way it's done." Gifft et al. state:

> Because man internalizes his cultural traditions, they become an inseparable part of him; few people realize to what extent they are both beneficiaries and the victims of the cultural traditions in which they were raised. (1972:11)

Oftentimes, the full magnitude of the influence that food has on a group is less likely to be recognized by a member of that group. Sometimes anthropological analysis of foodways goes well beyond the average community member's ability to recognize or articulate it. Brown and Mussell state that the members of a group do not necessarily recognize these meanings and premises when they are stated explicitly, because enculturation is "...a coming-to-acceptance of shared subtle meanings, or a taking-for-granted of the underlying criteria of a culture" (1984:12).

# Food, Friendship, and Communication

Food is a universal medium for expressing sociability and hospitality. Fieldhouse asserts that the closeness of social relationships between people can often be ascertained by examining the types of foods and meals they share together. For example, a new neighbor may be invited for coffee and doughnuts; casual acquaintances attend a cheese and wine soiree; business associates are offered a buffet; close friends are invited to sit down and share a full meal (1986:82). Fieldhouse, citing Mary Douglas (1972), comments that a cocktail party that offers food is a bridge between the intimacy of meals and the distance of drinks. Food and drink are a part of most social functions, and even of more formal meetings—albeit only coffee and doughnuts. The act of eating together indicates some degree of compatibility or acceptance; food is offered as a gesture of friendship. Oftentimes, the more elaborate the fare, the greater the implied intimacy or degree of esteem. Offering to share food is to offer to share a bit of oneself; to refuse food when offered can easily be seen as a rejection of friendship. To accept an invitation to a social function and then to refuse the food is viewed as unacceptable behavior (1986:82).

# Food as Language

According to Brown and Mussell, the use of structuralism, in which foods
are categorized by a set of classificatory principles, can be a great aid in the
study of foodways (1984:12–13). Binary oppositions (such as hot/sweet,
raw/cooked) are combined with syntactic rules that govern the combina-
tion of foods to create a "grammatically correct meal." Structuralism origi-
nated in the work of Ferdinand de Saussure and has been developed in the
writings of symbolic anthropologists such as Mary Douglas, Clifford Geertz,
Marshall Sahlins, Roland Barthes, and of course Claude Lévi Strauss. In
order to understand the coded meanings of a cultural system, structuralists
seek to treat these systems as languages and to analyze them by methods
and models borrowed from linguistics. As Lévi Strauss points out:

> ...we can hope to discover for each specific case how the cooking
> of a society is a language in which it unconsciously translates its
> structure—or else resigns itself, still unconsciously, to revealing
> its contradictions. (1966:595)

Another theory of food symbolism, espoused by Mary Douglas, is the
notion that food is meaningful in groups, whether in the form of meals,
feasts, categories of foods, or groups of foods. To Douglas, food categories
and groups encode social events because the groupings of foods are "...an
inevitable by-product and reflection of the rules and structure of a society's organization on both broad and intimate levels" (1972:61).

Structuralists use structural linguistics to decode this belief system and
discover the deep structure of meanings beneath surface communication.
In her extensive analysis of foodways, Mary Douglas writes:

> If food is to be treated as a code, the message it encodes will be
> found in the pattern of social relationships being expressed. The
> message is about different degrees of hierarchy, inclusion and ex-
> clusion, boundaries and transactions across boundaries. (1975:249)

Because foods and groups of foods are structurally reflective of social
rules, conditions, taboos, and boundaries, and because they implicate the
symbolic and material conditions of society, their careful analysis can reveal much about the culture being studied. It is important to carefully examine the many conditions and factors present within a given community
of individuals that come to shape culture. To do this, a comprehensive
study of the cultural milieu of the group in question is especially essential.
To best evaluate how a group's cultural attributes have come to be and
what they may become in the future, one must first examine what factors
and circumstances first influenced them.

# Food Traditions of Norway in Historical Perspective

In order to understand how Norwegian-American foodways have developed into what they are today, it is important to assess the food culture of Norway that was already in place at the time of emigration to America. According to KOM Forlag, an academic publisher of several Norwegian cultural works, people ate what they had, not necessarily what they liked. Fish, dried meats, milk, and grain were the mainstays of the winter diet. There was also a lot of porridge and bread. It is an interesting curiosity that there is no single-word translation for the Norwegian *pålegg*, which means "something put on bread." While bread elsewhere is an accompaniment to meat, fish, and cheese, the Norwegian meal consists of bread with something on it (1995:6). Forlag uses the popular Norwegian dish *får i kål* (lamb and cabbage stew) as an analogous symbol of Norwegian food culture:

> ...gathering around a steaming pot of lamb and cabbage stew tells a lot about Norwegian food culture. Not only is this dish a favorite, it also represents the importance of coming together for a good meal. Gathering around a table at home or with friends is an important part of Norwegian food culture. (1995:6)

Hospitality has always been an integral aspect of Norwegian-American culture. It seems Norwegians have always prided themselves in being warm, friendly, and hospitable. As Forlag states:

> For centuries, it has been the custom to offer the guests the best the house can offer. At holidays and celebrations, the home is

31

the gathering place.... Real Norwegian hospitality means inviting
guests into our homes. (Ibid)

The kitchen very much seems to be the center of the Norwegian-American
home, and food and the persistence of food culture is of paramount importance there. Bent Vanberg, a Minnesota author who has written about
the customs, culture, and culinary achievements of Norwegians, has
stated that no self-respecting Norwegian housewife would dream of being caught with her rolling pin down or less than seven different kinds
of cookies in her jars. Some are still hoping to bake fourteen varieties,
which, according to the old customs, equates to one kind for every day of
the whole Christmas season (1970:81–82).

## The Seasonality of Norwegian Foodways

According to Forlag, the fact that the Norwegian kitchen is seasonal is
only natural, considering the country's geographic location and the dramatic changes that each season brings. Norway is a long, thin country
with great variations both in the landscape and the climate. Measured
lengthwise, almost half of Norway lies above the Arctic Circle. The moun-
tains that separate the eastern and western parts of the country also delin-
eate the climatic differences between the two regions (1995:6).

During the winter, much of Norway is covered with snow. Historically,
this has meant that the entire summer is dedicated to gathering and stor-
ing food for the winter. This situation is not exclusive to Norway, but is
especially important there because of the climate. It used to be absolutely
necessary to secure enough food to last through the winter for the sole
sake of survival. A poor crop could mean near starvation for both family
and animals by springtime.

## Fish, the Backbone of Coastal Society

Traditionally, fish has always been a vital food source for Norwegians. In
their book about Norwegian recipes, history, and folk art, authors Louise
Roalson and Joan Liffring-Zug Bourret summarize Norwegian foodways as
"Fish, fish and more fish" (2003:81). Norway's terrain is mountainous and
rugged, with only very narrow strips of arable land. As Forlag states, the
small farms along the Norwegian coast were generally too small and un-
productive to feed a family, so naturally the people learned to rely on the
sea for their food. For the people along the coast, their "life rhythm" was
connected to the seasonal harvests of cod, herring, and mackerel (1995:10).

Roalson and Liffring-Zug Bourret assert that the American immigrants missed the saltwater fish of their homeland—the cod, salmon, herring, and mackerel. Dried foods were not as common in America either, so *lutefisk*, which requires dried cod, was seldom served. New types of freshwater fish, caught from local lakes and streams, were now the norm in America. Such fish was usually boiled and served with melted butter. Oftentimes, this fish ended up in *fiskesuppe* (fish soup), *fiskeboller* (fish balls), or *fiskepudding* (a baked mixture of flaked fish and cream sauce) (2003:82).

Fish has always had a special place in the Norwegian diet. Historically speaking, dried fish was especially important, both for trade and the table (Figure 2). Forlag has written that when Christian IV was crowned in August, 1596, rumors spread regarding the coronation feast. The "shopping list" included the following quantities of dried fish: 30,000 flounder, 24,000 whiting, 400 skates, 200 ling, and 12 barrels of preserved fish (the kind that was exported from Bergen):

> The sea has always been a stable source of food for people along the coast. Even if other food was scarce, they could always catch enough fish to survive. Fish for dinner two or three times a week is still the norm for the better part of the population. Along our long coast are some of the world's richest fishing grounds. It is no wonder that fish is more important in the Norwegian kitchen than in that of most other countries. (1995:10)

Figure 2. Washing salt fish. Many women were involved in the production of dried salt fish (Photo by Anders Beer Wilse, courtesy of the *Norsk Folkemuseum*, Oslo, Norway, retrieved from Forlag 1995:15).

Norwegians have high standards when it comes to fish, according to Forlag. Along the coast, fish could be prepared almost straight from the sea. Two things were important for a successful fish dinner: the fish should be firm of flesh and it should have no other taste than its own. Salt and vinegar were added; the salt to emphasize the flavor and the vinegar to keep the fish from falling apart during preparation. Even in today's kitchen, typical Norwegian fish dishes are known for their pure flavor, without the addition of other ingredients and seasonings that could diminish the flavor of the fish (Ibid).

Christie, who was a fellow kitchen worker at the Norsk Høstfest, has been attending the festival for the last several years to volunteer in the Scandinavian Kitchen. She stated that her main reasons for coming were for the sake of tradition and for the food. She talked at length about all the different types of food served at the festival. When asked why fish was so popular in traditional Norwegian food and persists among Americans of Norwegian ancestry today, she gave an unexpected answer. She made the point that Norwegians in particular need a diet that is rich in fish because it had been the main staple for countless generations, and they were culturally and genetically accustomed to fish products. As Christie states:

> We need a diet rich in fish, because it is in our genes to need fish products. Without fish or at least fish oils, Norwegian people just can't be healthy (Interview conducted on October 15, 2005; Minot, ND).

Forlag asserts that in Norway today, most dried fish is used to make *lutefisk*. He points out that this method of preserving fish goes back to the middle ages and gives a description from a 16th century volume. "Soak dried fish two days in a strong lye solution and one day in fresh water to make fine food" (Forlag 1995:13–14).

Most Norwegian Americans who still observe certain traditional aspects of their food culture enjoy at least one *lutefisk* dinner before Christmas. As Forlag states, "When passionate *lutefisk* fans gather around the table, it's one of the year's culinary highpoints" (1995:12).

In Norway, in the days before refrigeration, most fish was salted and air-dried in order to preserve it. This traditional process remained virtually unchanged for centuries, and it provided a stable source of food reserves for the Norwegian people. This process was done on a large scale, and during peak fishing periods, entire hillsides would be covered with the bounty of the sea (Figure 3). Obviously, fish was less plentiful in the landlocked Upper Midwest in the States. Consequently, the Norwegian immigrants had to turn to other more readily available food sources.

Figure 3. Stacking salt fish on the hillsides for drying. The fish was set out in the morning, and picked up again at night (Photo by Anders Beer Wilse, courtesy of the *Norsk Folkemuseum*, Oslo, Norway, retrieved from Forlag 1995:14).

# Butchering Time

Forlag has asserted that slaughtering was traditionally done in October and November in Norway. The animals were fat, and with the cold weather it was easier to store the meat. Superstition said that butchering had to take place during a waxing moon or a rising tide. Children and sick people were not allowed to be present during the butchering (1995:22).

Traditionally, everything was used, states Forlag, including innards, blood, and fat, but also calf stomachs, intestines, horns, hooves, skin, tendons, and bristles. Kidneys and liver were washed and rinsed. The kidneys were also blanched in boiling, lightly salted water a few minutes and then prepared. The head and other organ meats were soaked in cold, running water for twenty-four hours. Blood was never wasted. It was strained and then stirred until it lightened in color. Then it could be used in pancakes, blood pudding, sausages, and dumplings. The fat was trimmed, salted, and fried together with meat or fish. It could also be rendered into cooking fat and used in potato dumplings or blood pudding. Melted fat also could be mixed with lye to make soap (Ibid).

Roalson and Liffring-Zug Bourret write that the abundance of pork in America took some getting used to for many Norwegian immigrants. Back in Norway, pork had traditionally been only a Christmas treat, whereas in America, farmers seemed to have an abundance of pigs to slaughter. Bacon in particular was something that the immigrants were not at all accustomed to eating (2003:81).

# Breads and Other Staples

Bread, which was of utmost importance in the early days, was baked on a griddle or iron. Flatbread and *lefse* were the most important breads. At many meals, flatbread and *lefse* were served instead of porridge. Flatbread varied according to type of flour and thickness. To supplement and stretch the grain, potatoes often were used in the dough along with water, milk, or whey. For Christmas, the flatbread was rolled out thinner than usual.

Flatbread, Forlag asserts, was traditionally baked twice a year. This task was undertaken in the spring and just before or after slaughtering time in the fall. Normally, many farm wives got together to roll out sheets of flatbread on one large table. These baking women often traveled from farm to farm, carrying their own irons with them. According to Forlag, everyone needed a good supply of flatbread. "Flatbread was on the table for all meals—especially before the potato came to Scandinavia—and it was considered shameful to run out of it" (1995:25).

Flatbread dough, which was best made with freshly ground oats and water, was kneaded in a large trough. When the dough was stiff and thoroughly kneaded, it was divided into small balls of equal size that were then pressed into five-inch discs. These balls were rolled out with grooved or latticed rolling pins into thin round sheets about twenty inches in diameter and baked. Each sheet was rolled onto a thin wooden pin and then rolled out again onto a hot baking stone or griddle. The bread was baked lightly on both sides and then set aside to cool quickly, before it was returned to the griddle to bake completely. Then the sheets were stacked under light weights. When the stacks were completely cool, they were stored in the *larder* (Figure 4).

Figure 4. The *larder* was a storage house where provisions such as dried meats, *lefse,* and flatbread were stored (Photo by Per Eide, retrieved from Forlag 1995:23).

In addition to bread, porridge also has had an important role in the Norwegian diet, as it is cheap, easy to prepare, and nourishing. Forlag affirms that years ago people ate porridge at least once a day, often barley gruel served with sour milk (1995:24). Roalson and Liffring Zug-Bourret write of the importance of *grøt*, another type of porridge, among the immigrants:

> *Grøt* was a favorite food. This hearty porridge made by boiling milk with flour was the main dish for many a pioneer meal. Its Norwegian origin goes back to ancient times. If rich cream is used instead of milk, it becomes *rømmegrøt*, which is considered a treat in Norwegian homes today. (2003:81)

Traditionally, rice porridge was a standard feature of the national Christmas menu. Quite a few families served it early on the day of Christmas Eve with an almond nut mixed in. The lucky finder of the nut was awarded a special gift. According to Vanberg, for centuries in rural Norwegian folklore this porridge also had another very special purpose:

Every farm has its own little tenant, an elf called *nissen*, who resides in the barn and on a year round basis keeps an eye on everything and everybody. His annual reward is a bowl of rice porridge on Christmas Eve. If the bowl is found empty in the morning, all is indeed well, and the *nissen* has renewed his lease. If the porridge hasn't been touched, there is trouble ahead. The farmer could either take a chance and go on as before or emigrate to America. The good elf had apparently decided to move on to another farm. (1970:82)

Forlag has written that the potato is such a common ingredient in the Norwegian kitchen that it is strange to think that it has not always been available. It was introduced to Europe in the 1500s, and first arrived in Norway in the 1700s. When we know how difficult it was for people in Norway years ago to have enough grain for food, it is easy to understand how the potato quickly became an important part of their diet. Along with the potato, other vegetables such as the carrot, rutabaga, turnip, onion, and cabbage have the oldest tradition in Norwegian food culture (1995:26).

# Traditional Norwegian Foods that Were Never Brought to America

Much research has been undertaken in order to discover certain foods that are distinctly Norwegian yet are not found outside of the homeland. It is certainly an interesting and daunting task to document those highly authentic foods that, for whatever reason, never left Norway. Doing so can certainly bring about a better overall understanding of Norwegian-American foodways. Such documenting also serves to highlight how the realms of culture and environment overlap to produce distinct, localized foodways. Roalson and Liffring-Zug Bourret give some good examples of foods that are scarcely found outside of Norway. One of these is *gravlaks* (uncooked and marinated salmon). Traditionally, it was placed in the ground in its own "grave." Today, however, the salmon is covered with salt, sugar, and dill and put under a weight for several days. It is then served chilled in very thin slices (2003:87).

Reindeer meat is also very plentiful and is still on the menu in many restaurants in Norway. In the days before refrigeration and modern transportation, *spekemat* (cured and dried meat) was commonplace. Cloudberries, or *muelter,* are yellow berries that grow wild on mountain plateaus. They are rare, and whoever finds a patch usually keeps it a closely guarded secret. Lingonberries are similar to high bush cranberries in America (ibid.).

These foods were not available to settlers in the Upper Midwest of America, so the immigrants learned to substitute more readily available foods for those special foods. In so doing, the food changed little by little and took on its own distinct and regional flair. Because Norwegian-American foodways and culture are so closely integrated with one another, it is only natural that any change in one would directly correlate to a similar change in the other. In order to fully and properly assess this integration, it is vital to examine the settlement patterns of the Norwegian immigrants to determine not only where they settled, but also why.

# Demographics of Norwegian Americans in North Dakota

The following is a statistical representation of historical Norwegian-American settlement in North Dakota. The question we need to ask ourselves when examining Norwegian-American settlement patterns is, why did they choose North Dakota? According to William C. Sherman, a renowned ethnic historian, the answer to this question is simply that North Dakota was the only place left after Minnesota and Iowa. What Sherman means by this is that the Norwegian immigrants who settled in North Dakota, especially in the northwestern regions, for the most part had already been living in Norwegian enclaves in Minnesota and Iowa for quite some time (1988). These immigrants to North Dakota represented what Sherman termed "...'second bounce' immigrants. The majority were not right off the boat" (1983:36).

Sherman has written that thousands of Norwegian homesteaders flocked to the northern regions of North Dakota in the early 1900s. The highest concentrations of Norwegian settlers were found in the northwestern and northeastern regions of the state (1983). As Sherman asserts:

> Without question, Norwegians constitute the largest single ethnic group in the region. In fact the four counties that form the northwestern corner of North Dakota can be described as a Norwegian Sea with islands of other groups interspersed at random inside its boundaries. A venturesome soul could walk (with an occasional detour) from the Garrison Dam to the northwest corner of the state without stepping off Norwegian-owned land. (1983:36)

Although the Norwegian immigrants to the Upper Midwest shared a common language and geographic origin, they by no means represented a homogeneous culture. There were multiple groups with very distinct cultural inclinations who preferred each other's company over that of others. Norwegian immigrants, like most immigrants, chose to settle in close proximity to those who possessed the same dialect, clothing, foods, and festivals. According to Sherman:

> Residents of the Fort Ransom community in the late nineteenth century were divided into three groups: *Nordlendings* (North Norwegians), *Sorlendings* (South Norwegians) and *Eiris* (Irish, or those who couldn't speak Norwegian). The Fort Ransom division was not just a surface matter; the town boasted two Norwegian Lutheran churches, representing the differing sets of Norwegian cultural traditions.
>
> The divisions, matters of loyalty, show up elsewhere. Northwood in Grand Forks County was known as a Halling town, populated mainly by people from the great valley that traversed the central part of Norway between Oslo and Bergen. The Kindred community, and much of the northern part of Richland County, was also Halling in background. Brindsmade, in Benson County, is just one of the many towns that also attracted many from Hallingdal.
>
> The Stavanger area of Norway is reflected in the farmsteads around Cooperstown. Setesdal people are in the Walle Vicinity of Grand Forks County. Lesja people from Gudbrandsdalen, by way of Pope County, Minnesota, can be found in northern Bottineau County; Osterdalen natives took land in the Red River Valley, especially Cass County. People from Selby, while scattered around the state, went mostly to central and western North Dakota after spending several years in Minnesota. (1988:190)

As is evident from these many divisions, a great number of vastly different Norwegian groups were represented in the region, each with its own unique background and preferences. There were many issues of differing loyalties, as evidenced by the existence of more than one Norwegian Lutheran church in many communities. Nevertheless, Norwegians of whatever background tended to settle in close proximity to other Norwegians and form their own communities in the same way as other immigrant groups such as the Germans, Poles, and Irish (Figure 5).

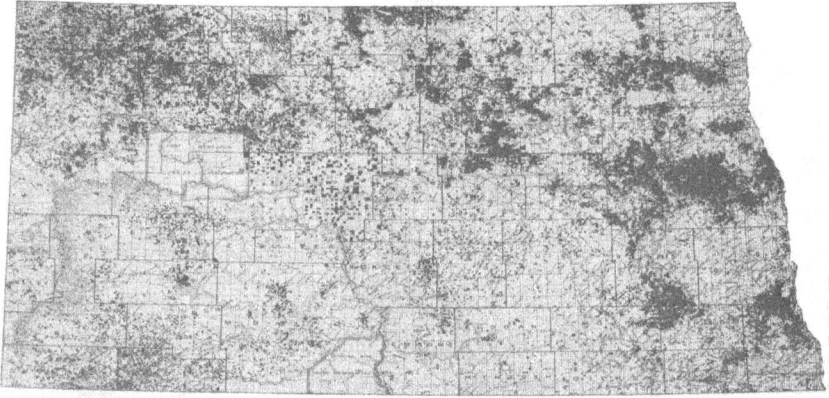

Figure 5. Land in North Dakota owned by people of Norwegian birth or descent in 1914, a total of 7,868,140 acres. The shaded acreage comprised about one-fifth of the farmland in the state of North Dakota (retrieved from Sherman and Thorson 1988:187).

# Traditional Norwegian
# Cultural Attributes Continued
# in the New World

Norwegian settlement patterns in the Upper Midwestern United States have certainly correlated closely with factors of geographic origin. However, it is vital to examine some of the more influential and enduring cultural factors involved as well. A number of Norwegian cultural tendencies and attributes have proven quite advantageous to the Norwegian-American experience in the Upper Midwestern United States. The concept of equality, which is regarded as such a vital tenet of American life, has seemed to come rather naturally to Norwegian Americans. As Roalson and Liffring-Zug Bourret state, equality has always been a treasured virtue among Norwegians. Showing off one's wealth, for example, is considered distasteful. Living with simplicity and being efficient are also highly esteemed qualities. In essence, "It seems it just isn't norsk to flaunt it" (2003:19).

Janet Letnes Martin and Suzanne Nelson characterize Norwegian Americans as frugal people who are not prone to doing things to excess. They go on to compile a short list of some of what, in their view, are the most prevalent Norwegian-American characteristics. Norwegian Americans can be characterized as "quiet, not touchy, introvert, Lutheran, white food, blonde" (1994:18).

Vanberg analyzes the extremely popular holiday, *Syttende Mai* (May Seventeenth), to illustrate Norwegian-American connectedness to

47

Norway. Though this celebration is a Norwegian holiday, commemorating the adoption of Norway's constitution in 1814, it is perhaps even more extensively celebrated in the United States and Canada than in Norway. Vanberg notes that the observance of this event may be more pronounced in North America simply because there are more Norse descendants here than in Norway. This may also be the case because the ties between the "Norway outside Norway" and the "Old Country" are in many ways stronger than similar relations between other ethnic groups and their respective ancestral countries. Vanberg writes, "The Norwegian immigrant is as fond of the Old Country as of his mother, and of the New Country as of his wife, and never is this unique loyalty so clearly expressed as it is on the 17th of May" (1970:77).

A great Norwegian immigrant story is found in *A Celebration of American Family Folklore* that clearly illustrates the extent to which Norwegian Americans embraced Americanism. Zeitlin et al., relate this story as remembered by Miriam Fors, age fifty-six, of Portland, Oregon:

> In nineteenth-century Norway a well-to-do governess fell in love with a poor farmer. The caste system discouraged marriage, but the governess was determined. In a burst of rebellious exuberance and a blue wedding dress, she married the farmer and sailed for America the same day, May Seventeenth, 1843. It was Norway's Independence Day.

> Their ship, the Tricolors, arrived in New York harbor on July Fourth, America's Independence Day. Here, as their great-granddaughter Miriam Fors tells it, "they were free to love each other."

> They moved from New York to Wisconsin where they built a log cabin. When the Civil War broke out, the farmer went to fight for the Union. His wife and young son longed for a flag to fly above their home, but American flags were scarce and there was little cloth to be had. So the mother and son took unbleached muslin flour sacks and made the white portions of the flag. Others were dyed red with Indian berries. But blue cloth was almost impossible to acquire.

> When there seemed no alternative, she took her blue wedding dress out of the large wooden trunk she had brought from Norway. And with tears in her eyes, she cut out the blue background for the white stars. Her son cut down a sapling tree, and the Norwegian immigrant family had an American flag to fly above their home. (1982:62)

This story is a clear representation of the enduring and cherished Norwegian-American theme of the patriotic, loyal citizen. What we must remember to focus on in this case, is not whether this story is true or not, but why this story and indeed scores of other stories like it, are told so frequently. The main reason, as I have asserted above, is that Norwegian Americans were and are as proud to be American as they are to be Norwegian. This story is an obvious representation of this. A unique dualism present in the Norwegian-American cultural identity somehow enables them to maintain the best of both worlds.

Perhaps one of the most prevalent Norwegian-American attributes is their durability, which has served them so well in the Upper Midwest. According to Sherman, this may be the chief reason why early Norwegian-American settlers stayed when many others left (1988:190). Sherman goes on to say that "some unique qualities must have been present in the Norwegian Character; they seem to have been almost predisposed to prairie life" (1983:92).

The Norwegian-American experience has certainly been both rich and successful. They seem to possess many noble and admirable qualities that, from the very start, have made them a true asset to this great nation. The numerous societal contributions of the Norwegian Americans are quite noteworthy, and certainly warrant celebration. It seems only natural that an event such as the Norsk Høstfest would develop as a timely and appropriate commemoration of Norwegian-American culture.

# The Norsk Høstfest

## Historical Background of the Norsk Høstfest

The Norsk Hostfest, founded in 1978, is North America's largest Scandinavian folk festival. Held in Minot, it celebrates the strong immigration ties North Dakota has to the Nordic countries of Norway, Sweden, Denmark, Finland, and Iceland. The four-day Hostfest primarily showcases the heritage and traditions of these countries.

Lori and Jim Olson have written that Høstfest grew out of the popular food and craft bazaars organized by the various Lutheran churches in North Dakota. One such pre-Høstfest celebration was organized by the Bethany, Zion, Christ, and First Lutheran churches of Minot, and featured festive *bunads* (Norwegian traditional costume), displays and demonstrations of Norwegian arts and crafts, and of course ethnic food (1995:15).

According to Lori and Jim Olson, Chester Reiten, who later became Høstfest president, along with a few of his friends, decided to continue the celebration as an annual event. They joined forces with a local chapter of the Sons of Norway and formed a foundation that produced the first annual Norsk Høstfest in October of 1978. The words *Norsk Høstfest,* literally translated, mean Norwegian autumn festival. This first annual Norsk Høstfest, held in late October, featured special prizes from Norway, a *rømmegrøt* eating contest, craft displays, music, and food provided by local churches. In fact, the Høstfest's biggest draw was the *lutefisk* supper (1995:16).

Today, ethnic food continues to be an integral component of the festival. In its first year, the Norwegian kitchen served seventy-five meals a

51

day, but by 1995 it was churning out one thousand meals daily for four days. Høstfest cuisine specializes in the foods eaten by Norwegian immigrants and their descendants. Some of the most popular foods are *lutefisk* (lye-soaked codfish; literally translated, "lye fish") and *lefse* (a type of potato flatbread). Typically, Høstfest serves five-thousand *lutefisk* meals and fifty-thousand slices of *lefse* each year. Other food highlights are Finnish stew and *kransekake,* a layered ring cake from Iceland (Courtesy of Local Legacies website, retrieved November, 2005).

Top entertainers, such as Bob Hope, Red Skelton, Barbara Mandrell, Victor Borge, and various Nordic performers, became a Høstfest tradition, helping to attract a wider audience from other states, as well as from Canada and the Nordic countries. The festival has also expanded from one day to five nights and four days. The first Høstfest attracted a few thousand visitors, but by 1991 sixty-thousand people attended. In 2005, the attendance was estimated at around fifty-five to sixty thousand people. But, even more than concerts, the Høstfest represents cultural heritage. The *bunad* show, showcasing the traditional costumes of the five Nordic countries, is among the most popular events.

In 1980, Høstfest established close ties with Scandinavia when Minot became a sister city to Skein, Norway. This relationship helped Minot play a small part in the staging of the 1994 Winter Olympics in Lillehammer, Norway. In 1983, Princess Astrid of Norway paid a royal visit to Minot. Her visit helped plant the seeds for the Scandinavian-American Hall of Fame, which honors Americans of Scandinavian background who have excelled in their chosen fields. The five Nordic countries, as well as Canada and the United States, are honored during a Parade of Flags ceremony (Local Legacies website, retrieved November, 2005).

Høstfest's Viking Market has grown to 120 exhibitors, of which each must have a Nordic flavor. Vendors and artisans are selected whose works provide a blend of familiar and unique items, from *rosemaling,* woodcarving, and computer-assisted quilt making to Scandinavian wool sweaters, jewelry, woven tablecloths, carved chairs, intricate needlework, and tatting (Høstfest 2005 Official Festival Guide).

## Cultural Context of the Norsk Høstfest

Based on the name and the theme of the Norsk Høstfest, one might automatically assume that the festival caters exclusively to individuals of Scandinavian heritage. This is only partially true. The Norsk Høstfest was originally founded as a festival celebrating Norwegian-American traditions. Over the years, however, the general population of North Dakota, which is also largely German, has become more widely represented there. The festival's theme is, after all, the celebration of the cultural heritage of immigrants to the Northern Great Plains. Therefore, it has become more commonplace to find other non-Scandinavian cultures represented there also, such as German and German-Russian culture (Figure 6).

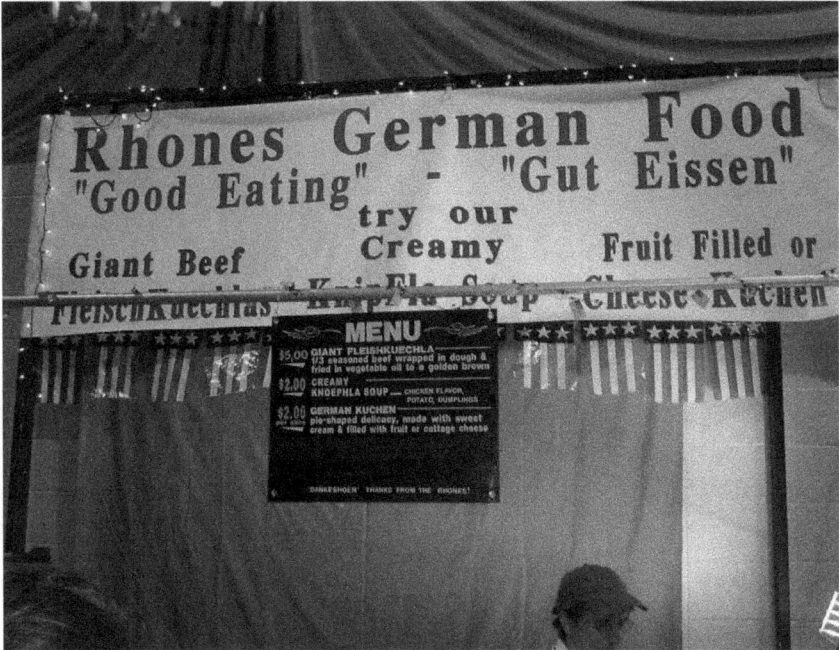

Figure 6. A food booth at the Norsk Høstfest advertising German specialties. Dr. Timothy Kloberdanz has pointed out that the German writing on the sign, "*Gut Eissen*," literally means "Good Iron." To be correct, it should say "*Gutes Essen*" (Good Eating) (Photo by Paul Emch, Saturday, October 15, 2005; Minot, ND).

The Norsk Høstfest started out as a small, highly localized festival celebrating Norwegian-American heritage. In the early years of the Høstfest, it was still fairly obscure, and did not exert much influence outside of the immediate Minot area. This has changed rapidly, however, as the festival has grown and grown, reaching epic proportions. The influence of the festival now extends throughout the rest of the United States, Canada, and the Scandinavian countries. Not surprisingly, its influence is most evident in the Upper Midwestern United States—so much so that it is not uncommon for people who have never even set foot in Minot to know about the Norsk Høstfest. The festival has inspired much commentary and publicity within the media, which represents possibly the foremost avenue for its expression and integration into Upper Midwestern culture (Figures 7 and 8).

Figure 7. A cartoon from *The Forum* (Fargo, North Dakota) that focuses on trolls, a prominent feature in Norwegian folklore. Trolls are a major theme at the Norsk Høstfest and, thus, are a symbol often associated with the festival (Courtesy of Dr. Timothy J. Kloberdanz and *The Forum*, Thursday, 13 October 2005:A11).

There has always been a strong sense of pride among the Norwegian Americans of the Upper Midwest, and this is a major theme at the Norsk Høstfest. In general, Norwegians are not given to showing off or being outwardly prideful. At the festival, though, their culture is showcased and celebrated with great enthusiasm. The Norsk Høstfest functions as a powerful symbol of Norwegian-American culture, and it serves as the one time each year when Norwegians can truly revel in their culture.

Figure 8. A cartoon from *The Forum* (Fargo, North Dakota) addressing the recent E. coli outbreaks. Here, once again, is another great Norwegian-American symbol, *lutefisk*, which is also closely associated with the Norsk Høstfest celebration (Courtesy of Dr. Timothy J. Kloberdanz and *The Forum*, Thursday, 12 October 2006:A11).

> The Norwegians of North Dakota deserve to be portrayed with respect and dignity. They have merited tribute. A century is not a long time of course, but it's long enough to create a chapter of Norwegian and American history. With nothing but physical strength and unyielding willpower, these people created a whole new society literally from the ground up in an empty, unfamiliar, and hostile part of the world. (*Western Viking*, August 26, 2005)

This sentiment rings especially true after reading the book *Giants in the Earth* by O. E. Rölvaag (1927). This book chronicles the life and times of a group of Norwegian-American families trying to make a life for themselves in the harsh Dakota Territory. It is a tale of hardship and woe that pits man against nature. This book really draws the reader in and helps one to appreciate the hardship and

trials of the first immigrants who sacrificed everything to tame this unforgiving land known as the Great Plains. The Norwegian Americans' story is one of survival and determination. It is only natural then that the Norsk Høstfest plays on this theme.

This festival is absolutely gargantuan. It is an annual festival that is scheduled in mid-October. It is held at the state fairgrounds in Minot, North Dakota, which currently seems just barely able to accommodate the huge crowds that flock to Høstfest.

## The Elderly Population

The Norsk Høstfest is attended by a predominantly elderly crowd with the average age probably falling somewhere around sixty. Christie, a fellow 2005 kitchen worker, commented on the question of why there were so few young people in attendance at Høstfest. She lamented that the festival really was not conceived with children or young people in mind. She gave a tragic example of this in a story about a child who got run over and killed several years ago at Høstfest because no one tends to be watching for children. Christie's view on why there were so many older people at Høstfest differed considerably from those of Kjersti, a Høstfest chef from Stavanger, Norway. Kjersti believes the reason the festival draws so many older people is that they represent the only cross section of society that has both the money and the free time to devote to this sort of festival (Figure 9).

Kjersti expressed regret that there were so few activities aimed at children and young people. She believes, though, that the Høstfest will by no means die out. As people grow older, she believes that cultural heritage becomes a more important factor, and that is what makes people want to attend the festival. So then, if it is the renewed enthusiasm for one's cultural heritage that motivates individuals to participate in this festival, and this enthusiasm tends to appear later in life, then perhaps the Norsk Høstfest is in no danger of falling by the wayside.

Lester, a middle-aged informant who attended the festival for the first time in 2005, also supports the assessment that one's heritage gains greater importance as one ages:

> That's a good point. I think it would. I mean, when I was eighteen to twenty, my heritage wasn't that interesting to me as it is now. And genealogy-wise, people that get involved in that would probably tend to be older. (Interview conducted on April 29, 2006; Grand Forks, ND).

Figure 9. Høstfest-goers congregate at the sidewalk café in Copenhagen Hall (Photo by Paul Emch, October 15, 2005; Minot, ND).

In his book about German-Russian settlers in the United States, North Dakota author Arnold H. Marzolf offers some very concise views concerning the value elderly individuals place on knowing who they are and where they come from:

> The older we become, the more important it is that we remember where we came from, who we are, whose we were, whom we served, and why we became what we are today. Some of those memories are of course sad, but most of them, I believe, are happy memories; some are even sacred. In other words, the present is seldom meaningful without the past, which gives the strength, courage, faith and hope to walk into the future. (1995:1)

It is easy for someone on the outside looking in to label the Norsk Høstfest as nothing more than a huge festival where a bunch of elderly Norwegians come together to reminisce about the good old days. Upon closer investigation, however, it has become more and more obvious that the Norsk Høstfest is the very embodiment of Norwegian-American culture clothed in festive form. Is it possible that the older generations see themselves as the gatekeepers of Norwegian-American traditions? This could very well be. If Marzolf's assertion is correct, that the past gives meaning to the present, then safeguarding the traditions of the past is of vital importance.

## The Norsk Høstfest 2005

The 2005 Norsk Høstfest, which was also the first Høstfest I attended for this study, was held exclusively in honor of Norway's centennial. In honor of this special event, the festival featured several very prestigious guests. The first guest was Princess Martha Louise of Norway, who gave special presentations on her book, *Why Kings and Queens Don't Wear Crowns.* Also in attendance was the Ambassador of Norway to the United States, Knut Vollebaek, and his wife, Ellen Sophie, as well as representatives from the Norwegian American Foundation. In conjunction with the Danes, the festival also observed the 200th birthday of beloved author Hans Christian Anderson. Norwegian entertainers also were featured, such as the renowned country music band the Kentucky Riders, Norway's award-winning dancer Karin Brennesvik, guitarist Thor Erik Falch and his daughter, Tove Lise, and country singer O. J. Hanssen, just to name a few.

In addition, the books, *Norway—Portrait of a Nation,* and *A North Dakota Story: Norwegian Footprints,* were offered for sale at Høstfest. There was also a Norwegian emigrant museum that encouraged people to bring photos and stories of their family's Norwegian roots to the museum. Representatives from Norway's only national museum were on the scene collecting and preserving Norwegian emigration data.

But, first and foremost, the Norsk Høstfest is about the food. Food has always been a major theme at the festival and is undoubtedly what draws many people to Høstfest. The new Brimli's Kitchen in Oslo Hall featured two new chefs in 2005, including the renowned Ståle Johanson, head chef at the legendary Fossheim Turisthotell in Norway, and Mark Norberg, an American chef who heads the Norway Pavilion at The Epcot Center at The Walt Disney World Resort. In the Scandinavian Kitchen in Reykjavik Hall, four returning chefs from Norway were joined by newcomer Kent Arntzen, food and beverage manager at Quality Hotel Mastemyr in Oslo, Norway (above information provided by the Høstfest 2005 Official Festival Guide).

# The Norsk Høstfest 2006

The major theme of the 2006 Norsk Høstfest was fine dining. The 2006 festival offered a fine dining experience in the form of the on-site restaurant *En To Tre*, an elegant culinary oasis located in Oslo Hall. *En To Tre* served excellent cuisine featuring meat, poultry, and seafood.

In Norwegian, *En To Tre* means "One Two Three," and the name symbolizes the three entities—Norsk Høstfest, Sons of Norway, and Norwill Scandinavian Gourmet Food Service—that teamed up in a dynamic partnership to make the restaurant possible. Two accomplished chefs oversaw the restaurant: Norwill's founder and head chef, Willy Hansen, and Ståle Johansen, head chef at the legendary Fossheim Turisthotell in Norway. The duo created the menus and were said to have prepared every meal, including the appetizer, main course, and coffee.

*En To Tre* was unlike anything ever offered at Norsk Høstfest, say festival organizers, and experiencing the atmosphere—let alone the food—proves it. It was a place to get away from it all, yet still be in the middle of it all, to enjoy a caliber of menu and cuisine usually found only in major cities, and to make new and exciting Høstfest memories.

The chief aspect of the 2006 Norsk Høstfest was of course the celebration of heritage. Chester Reiten, the Høstfest president, has written that an individual must understand his or her past to confidently move into the future. Furthermore, a people's past is their heritage and that heritage is the anchorage of life (Høstfest 2006 Official Festival Guide).

Reiten sums up his statements by reiterating that the foundation of Norsk Høstfest is the celebration of heritage. Heritage, he says, "is like a lighted torch passed from one generation to the next, and it is now up to us, the living, to continue to preserve, enhance, and pass on our heritage" (ibid.).

As always, the 2006 Høstfest featured world-class entertainment. Bjøro Haaland, the ever-popular Norwegian import, was back again that year bringing his music to loyal fans at Høstfest. Arve Tellefsen, also from Norway, delighted audiences with his prowess on the violin. The Kentucky Riders (yes, this group is from Norway) entertained audiences with their mix of country and pop music. Norwegian acoustic guitarists Steinar Albrightsen and Jørn Hoel blended their strings to make music that was twice the fun.

Peter Puma Hedlund, the world-champion musician from Sweden, entertained audiences with his skills on the *nykelharpa*, a traditional Swedish stringed instrument. And from Denmark, Harald Haugaard and Alfred Morten Høirup combined strings of the fiddle and guitar for a unique sound. In addition, there were Norwegian and Swedish dancers in native costume and vendors and chefs from all over Scandinavia.

Any Nordic visitors would most likely feel right at home at Høstfest: flags from Norway, Sweden, Finland, Denmark, and Iceland fluttered overhead, along with the U.S. and Canadian banners. The Halls of Høstfest bear the names of the great cities of Scandinavia: Reykjavik, Oslo, Stockholm, Helsinki, Copenhagen, and Trondheim.

You would not have to come from Scandinavia, though, to enjoy Høstfest's great Scandinavian-American marketplace, ethnic cuisine, and world-class entertainment. Stars for the 2006 festival included Liza Minnelli, Neil Sedaka, George Jones, Terri Clark, and the comedy duo of Tim Conway and Harvey Korman. Nearly every stage in the building held entertainment of some sort, and the halls and corridors of the building were often filled to capacity (above information provided by the Høstfest 2006 Souvenir Magazine).

Aside from all the big-name shows and scheduled entertainment, a plethora of other things occupied one's time at Høstfest. Food booths were selling every kind of Scandinavian delicacy imaginable. The smells that fill the buildings at the state fairgrounds are nothing short of mouth-watering. Along with the many fixed stands that sell everything from *rømmegrøt* to coffee, there are also many smaller mobile stands. These small, wheeled stands are pushed along by the vendors and peddle such delicacies as ring cake and *lefse*. It is fun to buy *lefse* this way, because along with your small Ziploc bag of *lefse*, you are also issued individual butter and sugar packets.

It was not very enjoyable to try to move around from hall to hall due to the congestion from the crowds. The mostly elderly masses seem to move ridiculously slowly, if at all. It was especially crowded after one of the big shows concluded, with all the people from the Great Hall flooding into the rest of the Høstfest concourse.

Another interesting feature at the Høstfest was the string of computer clusters lining the side of one hallway that offered free high-speed internet access. This computer area seemed to be frequented largely by the nontypical Høstfest-goers. I ran into one of the entertainers there, as well as some younger people, and a couple of Norwegian ladies who were chatting with each other in rapid-style Norwegian.

The festival truly has a way of bombarding the senses, and there is never a shortage of interesting things to observe or in which to participate. At the heart of it all is the Høstfest's overarching message, which is the celebration of heritage. This message is communicated through numerous manifestations and symbols of Norwegian-American culture—largely via the very tangible medium of foodways.

# Results

## Specific Symbols in Norwegian-American Foodways and Culture

One very powerful symbol associated with Høstfest, and Scandinavians in general, is coffee. The Høstfest 2005 Official Festival Guide even has a picture of a steaming hot cup of coffee on its cover. Alongside the cup of coffee is the slogan, "At Høstfest, the coffee is hot, the smiles are warm and now that you're here, the fun can begin!" Henrietta Oleson Bear in Roalson and Liffring-Zug Bourret, recalls, "Coffee was one of life's staples and no one came through our door without being offered a cup" (2003:83). According to human biologist Elaine N. McIntosh, Scandinavians are given much of the credit for perpetuating the American practice of coffee breaks, as well as many of the pastries that go with it (1995:185).

*Lefse*, which is the first of the two most widely known Norwegian-American foods, has always been a staple at the Norsk Høstfest. McIntosh has stated that in the Upper Midwest, *lefse* is a widely-accepted food even beyond the Scandinavian enclaves (1995:185). The second Norwegian-American food that is usually far less popular than *lefse* seems to take a special sort of person to enjoy eating it.

*Lutefisk*, the infamous food most often associated with Norwegian-American culture, also serves as a powerful symbol. It is my contention that *lutefisk* serves to symbolize the toughness and fortitude of the Norwegian people. A very good example of this symbol is in a story Lise Lunge Larsen tells in the video documentary *Tales of Minnesota*:

61

> Many years ago, the Vikings used to sail to Ireland to pillage. The
> Irish did not appreciate being pillaged at all, but what was worse
> was that the Vikings would steal and eat all their cod. The next
> time the Irish decided to dry the cod into rock-hard chunks, so
> the Vikings wouldn't want it. So the next year when the Vikings
> swooped through they found the rock-hard cod, loved it and ate it
> all again. After this, the Irish didn't know what to do. Then they
> got the idea that they should soak the cod in lye, hoping at least to
> poison them. So the Vikings came through again and pillaged and
> burned and when they found the lye fish they thought it was the
> best thing they had ever tasted. So the Irish said, "Why don't you
> take the fish and go to hell!" So that's what they did...and moved
> to Minnesota! (1987)

In any event, it would seem that the symbolism here is fairly self-explanatory. Only Norwegians could possess the resolve necessary to enjoy eating poisoned fish and living in a harsh place like Minnesota. Regardless of the fact that many people of Norwegian ancestry do not particularly like *lutefisk*, they will still eat it at least on occasion because it is such a strong traditional symbol of their culture. The message is this: "We are tough, and we have what it takes to survive in the midst of adversity."

In the quest to come to an understanding of the seemingly irrational *lutefisk* craze among Norwegian Americans, a particularly informative *lutefisk* story surfaced on a Norwegian jokes webpage of all places. This joke, posted by Gloria and Dean Peterson entitled "The *Lutefisk* Ritual," highlights a number of core characteristics of Scandinavian culture as they are tied in with the ritual-like consumption of the great cultural icon, *lutefisk*.

## The *Lutefisk* Ritual

The following is a parody of "A Night before Christmas"—as told by a Scandinavian who evidently hates *lutefisk*:

> Twas the day before Christmas with things all a bustle.
> As mama got set for the Christmas Eve tussle.
> Aunts, uncles and cousins would soon be arriving
> With stomachs all ready for Christmas Eve dining.
> While I sat alone with a feeling of dread,
> As visions of *lutefisk* danced in my head.
> The thought of the smell made my eyeball start burning,
> The thought of the taste set my stomach to churning,
> For I'm one of those who good Norwegians rebuff,
> A Scandahoovian boy who can't stand the stuff!
> Each year, however, I played at the game

To spare mama and papa the undying shame.
I must bear up bravely, I can't take the risk
Of relatives knowing I hate *lutefisk*.
I know they would spurn me, my presents withhold
If the unthinkable, unspeakable truth they were told.
Then out in the yard, I heard such a clatter;
I jumped up to see what was the matter.
There in the snow, all in a jumble,
Three of my uncles had taken a tumble.
My aunts, as usual gave what for,
And soon they were up and through the door.
Then with talk and more cheer, an hour was passed
As mama finished the Christmas repast.
From out in the kitchen, an odor came stealing
That fairly set my senses to reeling.
The smell of *lutefisk* crept down the hall
And wilted a plant, in a pot on the wall.
The others reacted as though they were smitten,
While the aroma laid low my poor helpless kitten.
Uncles Oscar and Lars said, "Oh, that smells yummy,"
And Kermit's eyes glittered while he patted his tummy.
The scent skipped on the ceiling and bounced off the floor
And the bird in the cuckoo fell to the floor.
Mama announced dinner by ringing a bell;
They pushed to the table with a yump and a yell.
I lifted my eyes to heaven and sighed,
And a rose on the wallpaper withered and died.
With leaded legs I found my chair
And sat in silence with an unseeing stare.
Most of the food was already in place;
There remained only to fill the *lutefisk's* space.
Then mama came proudly with a bowl on a trivet,
You would have thought the crown jewels were in it.
She placed it carefully down and took her seat,
And papa said grace before we would eat.
It seemed to me, with my whirling head,
The shortest prayer he'd ever said.
Then mama lifted the cover on the steaming dish
And I was face to face with that quivering fish.
"Me first," I heard Uncle Kermit call,
While I watched the paint peel off of the wall.
The plates were passed for papa to fill;
I waited, in agony, between fever and chill.
He would dip in the spoon and hold it up high;
It oozed onto the plate, I thought I would die.

Then came my plate and to my fevered brain
There seemed enough *lutefisk* to derail a train.
It looked like a mountain of congealing glue;
Oddly transparent, yet discolored in hue.
With butter and cream sauce I tried to conceal it;
I salted and peppered, but the smell would reveal it.
I drummed up my courage, I tried to be bold.
Mama reminds me to eat before it gets cold.
I decided to face it, "uff da," I sighed;
"Uff da, indeed," my stomach replied.
Then I summoned that resolve for which our breed's known.
My hand took the fork as with a mind of its own.
And with reckless abandon that *lutefisk* I ate,
Within twenty seconds I'd cleaned up my plate.
Uncle Kermit flashed me an ear to ear grin,
As butter and cream sauce dripped from his chin.
Then, to my great shock, he whispered in my ear,
"I'm sure glad this is over for another year!"
It was then I learned a great and wonderful truth,
That Swedes and Norwegians, from old men to youth,
Must each pay their dues to have the great joy
Of being known as a good Scandahoovian boy.
And so to you all, as you face the great test,
Happy Christmas to you, and to you all my best! (Retrieved January 2006 from http://www.lawzone.com/half-nor/lutefisk.htm)

The symbolism contained in this passage reveals much about the profound influence that food has on Norwegian cultural identity. For example, to reject *lutefisk* is almost seen as a symbolic rejection of one's own culture; this would be shameful because it could cause one to be labeled a "bad Norwegian." In a strictly traditional Norwegian-American family, especially a generation or so in the past, this rejection would be risky business. This passage also emphasizes "the resolve for which our breed's known." This resolve and toughness, as alluded to above, is a recurring core theme among Norwegian Americans. Also, interestingly enough, the "*lutefisk* ritual" seems to be a continual, if only annual, rite of passage for Norwegian Americans of all ages. It is referred to as the "great test," and all good Scandinavians are expected to "pay their dues" in order to be a bona fide member of "the group."

*Lutefisk* and *lefse* are cultural icons that would seem to be inseparable from Norwegian-American culture. Gary Legwold has described the art of making *lefse* as "a journey that helps define who I am. And the thanks for getting me started goes to *lefse*. The way back to Norway is through my stomach" (1992:3). Lori and Jim Olson assert that *lutefisk* and *lefse* are, in the same way, an inseparable part of the Norsk Høstfest as well. "*Lutefisk* and *lefse* are to Høstfest what hot dogs and peanuts are to baseball games—the event just can't be fully enjoyed without them" (1995:48).

# Milk Consumption as a Symbol of "Norwegianness"

*Lutefisk* and lefse are among the most obvious ethnic foods attributed to Norwegian Americans. Milk, however, which seems like such a generic and ordinary food item, also plays a very prominent role in Norwegian-American foodways and culture. Milk has been of vital importance to Norwegian Americans, both historically and currently. In general, Norwegians and Norwegian Americans love milk. Forlag states, that "Norway is a land of milk-drinkers. The average Norwegian drinks over 150 quarts of milk per year....Milk is a special drink in Norway, appreciated by both young and old" (1995:29–30).

In a 1994 article, Thomas Hylland Eriksen relates the totemic nature of milk within Norwegian culture in an examination of the Per Hatling Norwegian Dairies scandal. Per Hatling, the manager of a major dairy cooperative in Norway, was accused of some very questionable management practices. It seems he was out of touch with both the dairy producers and the consumers, who both valued dairy products as a national symbol rather than a commodity for capitalist exploitation. Apparently, Mr. Hatling did not fully understand the sacred importance that the Norwegian culture attributes to milk:

> The symbolic meaning of milk is apparent already in the design of the cartons. They feature a picture of grazing cows in one of those picturesque landscapes typical of 19th century national romanticism. There are also small stories on the cartons, intended for reading during breakfast, highlighting in different ways how milk is a natural and wholesome ingredient of Norwegianness.

> Other dairy products also have a central place in the Norwegian identity. Whipping cream is indispensable for birthday cakes all over the country. The brown cheese G35 won the competition for, "the most Norwegian of everything Norwegian" staged by a nationwide radio programme some years ago. "Real butter" is without question considered superior to both margarine and olive oil. Finally, one of the most famous advertisements in the country talks about Freia's milk chocolate as, "a little piece of Norway."

> Mr. Hatling has unwittingly violated a religious taboo in our
> society: Through his marketing strategies and his managerial
> style, he has turned the sacred drops of cow's milk into a glossy
> commodity...it goes without saying that an urban-minded no-
> nonsense capitalist like Per Hatling must fight in vain against a
> national totem of this magnitude. (1994)

Milk has been, and continues to be, important to Norwegian and
Norwegian-American culture for a wide array of reasons. In the words
of Eriksen, "Milk symbolizes health, the honest work on the land, the
beauty of the Norwegian scenery and—not least—pure whiteness. In
this latter respect, milk holds a position comparable to snow" (1994).
Sociologist Melanie E. DuPuis asserts that the apparent superiority
achieved by European dairying cultures during the American colonial
period was, in part, attributed to their dairy-based diet. She quotes the
famous nutritionist E. V. McCollum in National Dairy Council advertisements of the 1920s:

> The people who have achieved, who have become large, strong,
> vigorous people, who have reduced their infant mortality, who
> have the best trades in the world, who have an appreciation for
> art, literature and music, who are progressive in science and eve-
> ry activity of the human intellect are the people who have used
> liberal amounts of milk and its products. (2002:117)

According to medical anthropologist Andrea S. Wiley, "Not only was
drinking milk and consuming other dairy products seen as superior, it was
also viewed as normal and normative." In conjunction with this, there
has been a long-term trend in American culture of viewing milk-drinking
as extremely beneficial to one's health. "To consume milk in the United
States is to be healthy; to avoid milk is to put oneself at risk of a variety
of long-term ailments.... Drinking milk is no less than full enculturation
into U.S. life" (2004:514).

Kevin, an informant in his late thirties, related a very interesting story about the importance of milk in the Norwegian-American diet. This
particular story took place at his wedding, and involved his Norwegian-
American grandfather's unusual beverage choice there:

> There was champagne, wine, you know, everything else there
> that you could possibly want. When they asked my grandpa what
> he wanted to drink, he said "just milk." I'll never forget that you
> know, milk! (laughing) My grandpa, you know, he never touched
> a drop of alcohol in his life (Interview conducted on March 28,
> 2006; Fargo, ND).

True, milk would seem to be an important attribute of "Norwegianness." But to the Norwegian immigrants in America, it also served as a common bond with other European settlers who preceded the Norwegians. Since earlier settlers in the Northern Great Plains were also predominantly from dairying cultures, the process of acculturation may have been facilitated through mutual dependence on milk. Milk also served as a means of befriending the Indians, with whom the Norwegian immigrants interacted from time to time. Grandma Josephine, who is in her nineties, recalled her grandmother's stories about befriending the Indians by giving them milk, among other things:

> Grandma knew that the Indians liked tobacco and so she offered them some and befriended them. She also gave them milk, but not until Grandpa tried it first (Interview conducted on December 14, 2005; Mayville, ND).

Rölvaag also highlighted the importance of milk to the Norwegian immigrants in his book, *Giants in the Earth* (1927). The family milk cow was a treasured commodity to the Hansen family at every point throughout their Great Plains saga. Since they depended on the milk she provided for almost every meal, they took meticulous care of her. As they were making their sojourn across the prairies, their progress was determined in large part by the amount of traveling their beloved milk cow could tolerate. If they got too ambitious and walked her too far in a given day, she would subsequently give less milk.

Milk was obviously a precious commodity of survival both to the people of old Norway and to those making a new life here in the Northern Great Plains. For generations, Norwegians and Norwegian Americans alike have been enculturated to be milk-drinkers. Although milk is not the basic necessity of life that it once was, it still has a place of honor among those of Norwegian ancestry.

The role of milk at the Høstfest is not especially obvious, nor is it stated explicitly. The dairy company, Land O' Lakes, is a major sponsor there, and does have a stand that sells ice cream. However, there are no "milk stands," and no advertisements urging people to celebrate their heritage by drinking milk. Milk cannot be considered an ethnic food in this sense. Milk might more aptly be regarded as an ethnic ingredient, as it is a chief component in much of the food presented at the festival. The widespread use of milk and milk products in Norwegian-American foodways has resulted in its high level of integration within the culture. In this sense, it is understood that to partake in ethnic delicacies is to partake in dairy products—it is simply a given.

# What it Means to be Norwegian American

The ethnic foodways of Norwegian Americans certainly do convey numerous messages and sentiments that are especially emphasized at the Norsk Høstfest. Norwegian Americans, like any other cultural group, have certain beliefs, practices, ideals, and characteristics that set them apart from other cultural groups. It is precisely these cultural qualities that members of a particular culture come to embrace and celebrate as symbols of their culture. The celebration of these cultural qualities emphasizes cultural identity and group solidarity. In the context of a festival or celebration, those cultural characteristics that members of a particular group feel best represent the group are those that are most often showcased. They are celebrated and held up for all to see as a model of what the group putting on the festival is all about. According to Bass et al., "The success of a culture may be judged by the extent to which it meets the needs of its members" (1979:7). The assertion of cultural identity, and the sense of belongingness that comes with it, are fundamental human needs. Through analysis of these main symbols and themes, a more thorough understanding of Norwegian-American culture can be reached. Below is a short list of the main themes that have come to epitomize Norwegian-American culture and are represented at Norsk Høstfest for all to see:

1. Fellowship and Friendliness
2. Persistence of ethnic heritage
3. Norwegian-American contributions to American society
4. Strong work ethic and family values
5. The conflict between globalization and localization (this one is least obvious)

Throughout the interviews for this study, informants would often confess that they did not feel they would have much useful information to offer on this topic (What it means to be a Norwegian American). Perhaps this is a result of the inherent attitude of humility that is characteristic of so many Norwegian Americans. Maybe this is the case because so much of culture is unconscious. Grandma Josephine made the comment that "I don't think I will have anything very useful to tell you....I don't think I'm a very good Norwegian." When asked what she thought a good Norwegian had to be like, she replied, "Well, someone who knows all the facts and stories" (Interview conducted on December 14, 2005; Mayville, ND).

According to another informant, Lester, such a statement as this is to be expected and is, in fact, one of the chief markers of a good Norwegian. The norm among Norwegian Americans is to downplay all things relating to the self at all times, so as not to appear prideful. But yet, as he points out, it is a sort of false humility that is often stated explicitly, but seldom meant entirely.

> ...That's one of the key signs of being a good Norwegian is for them to say that type of thing....You know, it's humility in sum, but yet there's a bit of prideful humility in there. (Interview conducted on April 29, 2006; Grand Forks, ND)

Because of comments of this nature from Grandma Josephine and others in some of the interviews, it became apparent that what was needed was an assessment of the perceived prerequisites of being a "good Norwegian." This in turn gave rise to the standard question, "What are the characteristics of a good Norwegian?" This has proven to be a particularly useful approach, because it gets to the heart of those attributes that Norwegian Americans feel best represent their own culture. As one could well imagine, there were some very interesting responses to this question. Kent, a seventy-year-old officer from the Fargo Sons of Norway chapter, answered:

> Being healthy and strong, that's what I've always thought, and being intelligent. I think Norwegians are pretty intelligent, well Northern Europeans, I think all Northern....I shouldn't say that probably I suppose, but I think Northern Europeans are sharper than the world in general....I gotta be careful about that though, I could get in trouble (Interview conducted on April 6, 2006; Fargo, ND).

These themes or messages about what it means to be Norwegian American are present throughout the entire Norsk Høstfest, from the smallest *lefse* stand to the big-name shows. Are these themes, which are so prevalent throughout the festival, the same themes that are upheld daily to a greater or lesser extent by those who are of Norwegian background?

Vanberg asserts that Norwegian-American contributions to the development of America are innumerably vast. He points out that the many invaluable contributions Norwegian Americans have made to their adopted country have been amply acknowledged by historians and hailed by many of non-Norwegian descent:

> *President Abraham Lincoln:*...I know the Norwegians from Illinois, and I know that no immigrants have advanced America more than they...; *Governor Adlai E. Stevenson:*...The story of Norwegian settlement in the United States is rich in human interest and historic significance, withal, it is a peaceful drama in which

patience, courage, thrift and hard endeavor find fitting economic, political and cultural rewards....Throughout our republic, the
well-knit fabric of American society is far more colorful and im-
measurably stronger by reason of the strong strands woven into it
by men and women of Norwegian Blood.... (1970:34–35)

The preeminent Norwegian-American cultural attribute that seems to
continually resurface is that of full participation in American life. Among
other European immigrant groups in America, the Norwegian immigrants
seemed to be the first to try to assimilate. Sherman has asserted that
"no other large-sized North Dakota group seems to have had the ability
and desire to become American so rapidly, and at the same time, remain
loyal to its ethnic origins" (1983:38). Conversely, according to Sherman,
Norwegian immigrants were sometimes portrayed as "sell-outs" by other
groups because of their eagerness to assimilate (1983:20).

Bearing in mind all these cultural attributes enumerated above, one can
clearly see the character of Norwegian-American culture and why it has
developed in the manner it has. With this groundwork complete, there
is now a standard for comparing the input provided by the informants
through the course of the fieldwork.

# Discussion

## Fieldwork at the 2005 Norsk Høstfest

Throughout the fieldwork portion of this study, my informants have been both excellent and abundant. From native Norwegians, Minot residents, and people from the farthest reaches of the United States and Canada, they are all represented at Høstfest. One of the best insights on what the festival is like for those who call Minot home for the rest of the year was provided by Melissa. She is currently a student at NDSU and has a unique insider's perspective on how this festival affected both her and her family every year. When asked to describe the types of people who usually attend this celebration, she provided some excellent and concise insights:

> Most of the people are older, usually from their fifties and on. Most are also retired, which explains why they can afford to spend a whole week at the event. I don't think I am able to make a distinction if they are rural or urban, though. However, while there are a lot of locals that attend the event, most of them are visitors. The hotels are so full in Minot that many people rent out rooms in their houses to accommodate for all of the visitors. My family does this, and we have hosted a couple from Alaska for several years. It's pretty amazing. These people drive down from Alaska every year just to attend this event! (Interview conducted on October 26, 2005; Fargo, ND).

The most pressing question of this study is, of course, what the overall role of food is in the Norsk Høstfest celebration. Much research has been conducted in order to discover to what extent Høstfest

71

is a celebration of Norwegian food. When asked this same question, Melissa responded:

> Food plays a pivotal role in any cultural celebration, especially in this one. As I said before, our guests are always excited to share what they ate and their opinions on it. *Lutefisk* is a great example of the important role of food. Since it is a symbol of the Scandinavian heritage, everyone wants to try it. I volunteered one year in the *lutefisk* booth, and I was busy the whole three hours I was there. Everyone wanted to taste, smell, and see it. Even if they watched someone try it and tell them that it was disgusting, they still come and pay money for it. It never ceases to amaze me how curious people are about food. I think part of it has to do with the fact that food is really the only aspect of that culture that appeals to our sense of taste. So much of our focus is on our sense of sight in this celebration, so it is nice to appeal to another sense. (ibid.)

American folklorist Angus Kress Gillespie states that festivals are an affirmation and a validation of tradition bearers (1996:251). He asserts that the important thing to focus on is the festival's impact on the artists. This concept is perhaps the most relevant question that can be asked in regards to understanding a folk group through the analysis of an event. It has prompted one of the most pressing questions in this study: What does the Norsk Høstfest mean to different people who are involved in it? In addressing the question of what Høstfest means to different people, I turned once again to one of my star informants and Minot local, Melissa:

> For the longest time, it meant that I had to sleep on the floor in the living room for a week because my parents always rented out my room! But looking at it seriously, it really is a symbol of my community. People across the United States know where Minot, North Dakota, is because they associate the city with the Norsk Høstfest. And just seeing all of the volunteers every year really shows how much people care about the success of the event. It also means a chance to celebrate the Scandinavian culture. I would have never tried *lutefisk* without the Høstfest. So to me, it is a chance to look into the Scandinavian culture in full detail. (October 26, 2005)

Sven is a famous chef from Oslo, Norway, who has been coming to Høstfest every year since 1993. Back home, Sven works as head chef at a large hotel. Sven was the first native Norwegian I was able to interview for this study, and he provided some excellent information that has applied well to this topic. Since Sven was very busy in the kitchen, the only time he was able to really talk with me was during smoke breaks (Figure 10).

Figure 10. While the other chefs took a smoke break, Sven entertained the crowd with a demonstration of his bicycling skills (Photo by Paul Emch, October 15, 2005; Minot, ND).

As one could well imagine, the perceptions of Norwegians are much different from those of Norwegian Americans regarding this festival. It is important to remember that native Norwegians should by no means have the final word as to whether or not the Høstfest displays "genuine" Norwegian culture. After all, the Norsk Høstfest is principally a celebration of Norwegian-American culture. Bearing all of this in mind, it was, however, very enlightening to get the opinions of native Norwegians as to the "authenticity" of Høstfest:

> It's much different in Norway now than what it is portrayed as at Høstfest. You see that lady over there (gesturing), the one wearing that grey sweater? (indicating a woman wearing a sweater with a *rosemaling* pattern) You would look very strange walking around Norway wearing something like that now. (Interview conducted on October 15, 2005; Minot, ND)

According to Sven, the Norwegian culture displayed at Høstfest is the Norway of one-hundred years ago. Modern-day Norway is shopping malls and McDonalds and is much like America in many regards.

Kjersti, a chef from Stavanger, Norway, whom I have already introduced, offered a lot of input on the differences in food found at Høstfest versus the food of contemporary Norway. She said that while the food was basically similar, it was very much tailored to appeal to the mostly American crowd. For example, the *fiskesuppe* (fish soup) and the creamed vegetables contained no cabbage, which according to Kjersti is necessary for good, authentic Norwegian cooking.

Kjersti made one very humorous comment relating to folk speech. When I had introduced myself as an anthropology student from North Dakota State University in Fargo, she said:

> Oh Fargo, I know the place.... I have seen that movie called *Fargo* many times and it's one of my favorites. But I'm surprised...you don't have a Fargo accent. (Interview conducted on October 15, 2005; Minot, ND)

I got a good laugh out of this, and had to explain to her that the folk speech  stereotype portrayed in the movie *Fargo* was not quite accurate and was more of a joke—or at least an exaggeration. Then we talked more in depth about the pros and cons of Høstfest and why she felt the authenticity of the food suffers at the festival. She felt that the festival had just gotten too big and commercialized and this was in large part what caused the food to be somewhat lacking in authenticity. People come to the festival wanting what they perceive as traditional Scandinavian food, but in reality it is very much an Americanized version of Scandinavian food.

I asked Kjersti about the traditional dish called *rullepølse* (rolled, pressed sandwich meat) and if it was still made often in Norway. As Dr. Timothy Kloberdanz has stated, this dish is still made in North Dakota, especially in the Fort Ransom area. Kjersti said that *rullepølse* was very rarely prepared anymore in Norway, because it is so time-consuming and complex. She said that many Americans are interested in authentic Norwegian foods that are complex and difficult to make because they think those types of food are somehow the best. She believes that this just simply is not the case. There are many types of authentic Norwegian foods that are very easily made and yet are among the best to eat, according to Kjersti.

Joe, an elderly informant, said that he especially loves Høstfest for the people (Figure 11). Joe and his wife run a small crafts stand every year and relish the opportunity to meet a wide variety of people:

> I guess what keeps me coming back is all the nice people and all the friends we've made over the years....Well, when it comes down to it, I just couldn't justify not going anymore, because of

all the friends I've made here over the years....I guess that and all
the fun we have here too. (Interview conducted on October 15,
2005; Minot, ND)

Figure 11. Sven and Joe pose for a picture during a smoke break. The
reader will notice the sword-through-the-head hat that Joe is wearing.
According to Joe, this item is one of the many souvenirs that he and his
wife sell at their stand (Photo by Paul Emch, October 15, 2005; Minot,
ND).

According to Joe, who made a pilgrimage of sorts to Norway a couple
years ago, the food you tend to get in the "Old Country" is quite a bit different from that at Høstfest: "Yeah, it's different there from what you can
get here. When I was in Norway, there was a lot more fish on the menu.
Yeah...it was salmon for every meal! (laughing)."

The festival area was absolutely packed when I was there in October
of 2005. Visitors, many of whom seemed old enough to remember Pearl
Harbor, strolled around the displays. Many people buy Norwegian sweaters
and eat Norwegian delicacies such as *lefse* and ring cake. Some admire the
wood carvings and *rosemaling*, while others listen to the Norwegian music.
Others simply like to sit around and discuss anything and everything. The
halls of the State Fair complex are packed with people at almost any given

time during the festival. There are people milling around continuously from morning until night, talking, admiring the displays, and coming or going from some show or another. For the most part, people just like to stroll through the halls without a care in the world. The atmosphere is, in a word, very congenial. According to Linda, a pleasant elderly informant, festival organizers describe the crowd as "sixty-thousand friends you haven't met yet," (Interview conducted on October 15, 2005; Minot, ND).

Quite a few of the people I spoke to alluded to the overall feeling of warmth at the festival. Christie stated, "It's very friendly. You can be in a hallway jammed with people, and you just start talking with anybody" (Interview conducted on October 15, 2005; Minot, ND). When asked for her assessment of the festival, Jackie responded in great detail:

> Everyone there just seemed so willing to tell you everything they know. And they're like so excited to be there and to share everything they know about that, about their heritage, it's just like everyone feels excited when they're there...I expected it to be just like this boring thing with like, older people. That's why I never went even though I lived so close. But I really liked it and I wanna go back and just enjoy it. And I don't know, it was pretty fun and you get to experience so much of the different ranges, and the different culture from the different people, with the food and the music and the entertainment. It seems like people are like, smiley and happy—it just feels good to be there, I guess... it's just like the second I walked in the door I felt bombarded by the smells...and the music and the people, and the—everything you see, it's just like your senses are all bombarded at once by all these things....I think maybe that's part of why it's so stimulating you know, especially to someone like me, it's like I've never really been—I mean I've been around that stuff, cause I grew up in this area, but never really paid attention to it or really appreciated it or anything. It's kinda cool to take it all in and absorb everything. (Interview conducted on March 23, 2006; Fargo, ND)

Marianne, an older lady who has yet to miss a single day of Høstfest, stated that "you meet people. That is what's so much fun about the Høstfest; there are no grouches here" (Interview conducted on October 15, 2005; Minot, ND). The Norsk Høstfest is filled with happy, friendly people who seem to be thoroughly enjoying themselves. It could be described as a Norwegian atmosphere reduced and simplified so that everyone can identify with it. It certainly does not take long for people to feel as if they belong there, no matter what their ethnic background is.

# Fieldwork at the Fargo Sons of Norway Lodge

At the conclusion of the 2005 Høstfest, I returned to Fargo to undertake further research. As it turned out, one of the best places in the area for gathering information about Norwegian-American culture is Fargo's Sons of Norway Lodge. Fargo's "Kringen Lodge" is a place where Scandinavian fellowship takes place several nights per week. In this way, Kringen Lodge is much like the Norsk Høstfest in miniature (Figure 12). The first Sons of Norway event I attended was the long-awaited accordion concert by Kringen Lodge's own accordion band. In all honesty, I have never really been enthralled by "squeeze-box" music. Although it is also a cultural icon from within my own German heritage, and in league with such national treasures as *Sauerkraut, Kuchen,* and *Oktoberfest,* I cannot bring myself to enjoy it much. This is probably true of most people of the younger generations.

Putting all that aside, however, the accordion concert was both interesting and enjoyable. More importantly, though, this event offered much to analyze and ponder. David, the accordion band leader and M.C. for the evening, told jokes and introduced the songs. His jokes and stories naturally dealt with Norwegian-American heritage. And what could be more fitting than a good Norwegian joke about *lutefisk*?:

> We have *lutefisk* dinners six times a year [at Kringen Lodge], and although there's nothing scientific about this, um, a guy that's on the staff at Bethlehem Lutheran told me this, so it must be true. He said, um, if you eat enough *lutefisk* you don't need to take a flu shot! (April 4, 2006; Fargo, ND)

This joke brings to light more *lutefisk* symbolism that really serves to accent some of the references already made to *lutefisk*. The themes of toughness and fortitude once again come to the surface. Could David be hinting that *lutefisk* is good medicine for Norwegians? Does this type of joke reflect the old saying of "what doesn't kill you only makes you stronger?" (Though this expression cannot be positively attributed to Norwegian-American culture, in this case it succinctly illustrates the point.) The reader will also notice the reference to the Lutheran Church. In the following quote, which is another joke told by David, the Catholic Church comes out as the indirect butt of the joke:

Figure 12. Here is a close-up photo of the Sons of Norway shield. Emblazoned at the top of the shield is the North Star, which guided many a Norse sailor by night. In the foreground is the Viking *langskip* sailing the rolling sea in the shadow of the midnight sun (Photo by Paul Emch, April 4, 2006; Fargo, ND).

> Well, there was a guy who came into the bar, and he sits down, muttering to himself. The bartender comes over and he says, "You look like you've had a tough day, what'll ya have?" "Whiskey!" he says, "but wait, first can I ask you something?" So the bartender says, "Well, sure." "How tall does a penguin get?" Bartender says, "Well, uh, about two feet tall." "Oh, you better bring me a double." So the bartender does and the fella downs it all at once. "How tall can a penguin get?" he asks again. Bartender says, "Oh maybe two, two and a half feet maybe." "Are you sure? Is that all? Oh, you gotta bring me another double then!" The bartender brings him his drink and he puts it down quicker than the first. Well, um, after a couple of minutes, the fella asked the bartender again, "Okay, tell me one more time, how big does a penguin get?" He says, "It's like I told you, two and a half, maybe three feet tall." Fella says, "Oh, lord, guess that musta been a nun I ran over then."

This joke illustrates, once again, the underlying tension that still exists to some extent between the Catholics and the predominantly Lutheran Norwegian Americans. The accordion social yielded a lot of good information, but the Sons of Norway Lodge meeting later that week produced even better material.

To open the meeting, the president had everyone stand and sing a collection of patriotic songs, including; "Oh Canada," "*Ja, vi elsker dette landet*" ("Yes, We Love This Land of Ours" [the Norwegian National Anthem]), and then, rather enthusiastically, the "Star Spangled Banner," followed by the Pledge of Allegiance. Norwegian-American heritage seems to be indelibly linked to the spirit of patriotism and an affirmation of being good American citizens. This theme is very much evident both at the Sons of Norway Lodge, and the Norsk Høstfest. At the end of the accordion performance, as yet another marked pronouncement of American pride, the musicians played "God Bless America," to which the crowd heartily sang along. This seemed to be a very public display of patriotism and American identity, which Norwegian Americans by and large take great pride in.

Two nights after the accordion concert, I interviewed a very congenial, elderly couple at the Kringen Lodge meeting. We were discussing their views on Norwegian-American culture, and, as is often the case, the topic of Norwegian hospitality came up. The Olsons recounted the story of their trip to Norway a couple years ago. As Mrs. Olson recalls:

> ...We went to one house...they had two kinds of cake, and they served us coffee. They like to entertain, they like to entertain, I

mean, I think Norwegians just like to entertain. I think that comes
from Norway, you know. Well, their weddings last for two days!
(laughing). (Interview conducted on April 6, 2006; Fargo, ND)

The hospitality factor was one that the Olsons seemed to really identify
with. The way they described it made it clear this was something that was
highly significant to them, and a quality that they personally strive to uphold.

Toward the end of the interview with the Olsons, I decided to quiz them
on the question of what makes a good Norwegian. This question seemed
to thoroughly amuse them. Mrs. Olson, who was caught somewhat off
guard by this question, replied, "What makes a good Norwegian?! (laughing)." With a grin, Mr. Olson said, "You gotta be dumb. You know they
always say, a dumb Norwegian...!" I asked him if that is why so many
Norwegian jokes are told, and why, ironically enough, it seems to be
mostly Norwegians who tell many of these jokes. He replied, "Yeah. What
culture has so much fun with their own people as the Norwegians...I
mean, telling jokes? The Poles come in next, I guess."

We addressed some of the differences between how people act at the
Norsk Høstfest and how they act in everyday life. Once again, the Olsons
called upon their experiences in Norway for examples. Mrs. Olson stated,
"Yeah, well, the Norwegians, when they have something, they really have
it, a feast or whatever." She made it clear that people in Norway can just
decide to have fun at the drop of a hat. They do not necessarily need a
large festival, or a lot of alcohol, they just "let it all hang out." As an example, Mr. Olson compared Norwegians with Norwegian Americans in
the context of a Sons of Norway activity:

> Well, you take the Sons of Norway. Now people in Norway they
> just let their hair down, you know, "Let's go to it." But here we're
> so sophisticated you know. The whole problem with this club
> here is that everyone's just too sophisticated...and that's too bad.

I asked them if they thought perhaps the Norsk Høstfest was the kind of
place where people could really just let loose—a place where, for a short
time, one can put all stoicism aside and celebrate. They both emphatically
agreed with this assessment. Mrs. Olson affirmed, "Yeah, yeah, you can
really just let your hair down there."

## Fieldwork at the 2006 Norsk Høstfest

The countless hours of fieldwork I had undertaken subsequent to my
research at the 2005 Norsk Høstfest had taught me a lot and revealed
much about the nature of Norwegian-American culture. I also felt I had

a relatively complete understanding of the structure and workings of the festival. Nothing, however, could have fully prepared me for what I was to discover at the 2006 Norsk Høstfest.

On Thursday, October 12, I conducted a face-to-face interview with a highly influential Høstfest organizer, Charlie. He was very instrumental in organizing the first festival in 1978, which later became the Norsk Høstfest. He was possibly my most outspoken informant to date, and was able to clear up some common misconceptions and "set the record straight." From the start, Charlie impressed on me that he did not wish to discuss Norwegian-American foodways, but rather other cultural aspects. Regrettably, at times he even made comments marginalizing the role of food at the festival. Nevertheless, he still did contribute greatly to this study. The reader should bear in mind that though Charlie does have a unique and central position in all of this, his is still only one perspective. I do not by any means assert that he is the final authority on Norwegian-American culture or even the Høstfest itself. His words should be taken with a grain of salt, as with any other informant.

I was shown into his office, which was little more than a small room with a desk, a chair, and a pair of recliners. There was the aging Høstfest organizer, sprawled out in a blue leather recliner in the corner. After a brief introduction, I took a seat next to him in a matching blue recliner, and the interview began. To start off, I asked him how the Norsk Høstfest got started, and where the idea came from in the first place. To be sure, his response surprised me:

> ...Okay, the model of this thing...was based on a typical Saturday night in a small town. People would bring their cream and eggs to town, and then they would shop, and then they would get entertained, and then they would end up in the restaurants—the men stood on the sidewalk, and the women sat, and they talked, and they visited. Now all this is an application of that whole thing. There is nothing new. This is just a Saturday night in North Dakota, fifty years ago. So it's a proven idea...it was not a new idea, it already existed. We just expanded it, so that instead of having a hundred people, we get fifty-thousand. But that is why we use the "hi and where are you from?" [a Høstfest motto] It gets people to visit. The Scandinavians, basically—and the Germans are the same way—they are not going to slap you on the back and ask your name. You can get by asking "Well where are you from?"... and then you talk...the visiting is a big part of [Høstfest]. (Interview conducted on October 12, 2006; Minot, ND)

Up until this interview, I had never even heard a mention of this festival being based on a "Saturday night in North Dakota fifty years ago." This sentiment illustrates a perfect example of how localization is represented within this festival. This model is a North Dakota thing—and more specifically, a Minot thing. It gives the Høstfest its own distinct, regional personality. I had certainly never heard anything quite like this from any of my informants to date, and frankly, the idea had never even crossed my mind. If anything, I thought it might more likely be modeled after a family gathering on a grand scale.

Then I asked him how he thought Høstfest helps to link local and perhaps international audiences. He replied:

> Yeah, we had a guy put on [a presentation] today, Carol Juven, [head of the Juven tour company which charters tours of Norway] from Fargo. He's sent one hundred and twenty bus tours to Norway, twenty-thousand people!...We had a banquet last night, with five-hundred people there, and four-hundred were from Scandinavia. That's them getting to know us, and us to know them....The way you're going to finally have peace is for people to know people. So we go to Norway, and have been there many times. You get to know the people and then they come here.

The concept of peace coming through people getting to know people, as Charlie has stated, is a very valid point. It is good to cultivate relationships with individuals from around the world and get to know them and understand their way of thinking. Knowing and understanding people from other cultures and traditions is the hallmark of diplomacy and indeed cultural anthropology. It may very well be the one factor that will bring about mutual understanding and a lasting peace. The U.S. certainly has no bone to pick with Scandinavia, of course, but the benefit of this concept of people knowing people is quite valid, nonetheless.

Another thing that really surprised me was Charlie's comments on how the Høstfest got started in the first place. Based on much of what I had heard and read up to this point, I was under the impression that the Norsk Høstfest was started by a number of local Lutheran churches. Charlie quickly and emphatically contended this notion:

> It had nothing to do with that, it's completely wrong! (slapping the sheet of paper in his hands). They're trying to tell you that. The Lutherans, and I'm a Lutheran too by the way, they had food festivals before, but *no!* (slapping the sheet again) *We* started it! And then we had them come in and sell food. It wasn't started by them! I'm just telling you this for your [thesis], you know. I was the one who started it, and a few other people back when I was mayor. I know you'll hear that, but they have their booths, and they make a lot of money off us. But they *did not* start it! Most

of us were Lutherans, but it was not the church, it was not the preachers, nothing like that. It was the leaders of the community.

Although Charlie has so emphatically denied the contributions of the Lutheran Church to the Høstfest, I still maintain that church influence was and still is quite significant there. It is safe to say that the main idea for the Høstfest originally came by way of the local Lutheran Churches. According to Lori and Jim Olson, Høstfest organizers and community leaders based the very first Høstfest on the church-sponsored ethnic food and craft bazaars that were very popular prior to this festival (1995:15–16). Charlie begrudgingly acknowledges the strong presence of the local Lutheran churches at the festival, chiefly in the area of food vending. He seemed somewhat irritated by the fact that the churches "...make a lot of money off us," and this may partially account for his minimization of the role of food at the festival.

From the beginning of my field research at the Norsk Høstfest, I knew that it catered to a largely older crowd. It only takes one look to see that the vast majority of attendees are fifty years old and above. What I did not realize is that this particular age group is specifically targeted, while anyone else who falls below this age group is effectively excluded. Charlie stated:

> We're not going to alienate the people who are fifty plus, to get the thirty-five year-olds. I can tell you that from my experience with radio and TV—you can't mix the two. People say, "Well, you gotta get the young people." Well fine, if you get the young people, and these people (gesturing) will leave. No, the young people can go to the "We Fest" [a large, Country music festival]. I don't know why we have to be so worried about the young people for, they have all that stuff. Well what about the senior citizens?

Charlie was very adamant on this point, and in my opinion, even slightly defensive at times. Whether he was simply trying to convince me of his point, or merely on a rant, he kept driving this point across:

> Make no bones; it's a senior citizen thing. And like I told you, everybody says "*Ooh*, gotta get the young people." Not interested. When we started twenty-nine years ago, well, most of those people are dead. Then they said, "*Ooh*, when they're dead, you won't have any heritage." Here, it's up to fifty-thousand. You see, they come up. They come up as soon as they get the first grandchild—now they're interested in heritage. You see, they say you have to get the young people. No, you see, they'll come when they're fifty.

I asked Charlie if, in his opinion, heritage becomes more important to people as they get older. He replied, "Much more! And you've got grandchildren, and you're out of the pressure of life, so you can come here."

There is a fascinating parallel that can be drawn between what Charlie has said regarding grandchildren and Marcus Lee Hansen's three-generation model regarding immigrant groups. This model, known as "Hansen's Law," describes the process by which heritage is blatantly obvious among the first generation of immigrants, is spurned and repressed in the second, and finally comes to be rediscovered in the third (Hansen 1940; Timothy J. Kloberdanz, March 28, 2006, "Germans from Russia" course, North Dakota State University).

My interview with Charlie really opened my eyes to the existence of a real and ideal aspect of the festival. What I had read in the Høstfest 2005 and 2006 Official Festival Guides and what Charlie and I talked about contrasted rather starkly at times. There are several obvious differences even between how he described the festival and what I personally read about the Høstfest and witnessed there.

For example, Charlie made the comment "We don't sell beer" as a way of pointing out the differences between the Høstfest and other festivals that cater to younger people, such as We Fest. Charlie mentioned, somewhat disparagingly, how at We Fest forty percent of the profit is in beer sales. He seemed to take pride in the fact that the Høstfest is different from other festivals and events in this way. However, beer actually is sold at Høstfest and I had witnessed at least one place that sold any kind of beer you could want. Beer stands were certainly not the norm, though, as you would see at most any other festival or event in the state. I am quite certain that the beer sales at the Høstfest would pale in comparison with such giants as *lutefisk* and *lefse*, no matter how many beer stands there might be.

Looking back on this interview, it has occurred to me that perhaps Charlie's distain toward alcohol was also motivated by the influences of the Lutheran church. It would seem that many Norwegian Lutherans tend to have a somewhat negative view toward alcohol, and this in turn has come to set them apart from other groups. For example, Russell, a fellow kitchen worker who pastors both a Norwegian Lutheran church and a German Lutheran church, pointed out the very different viewpoints toward alcohol within these two churches:

> I've been pastoring for quite a few years now, and I've noticed big differences in the two churches. At the Norwegian church, they always told me, "We don't want to see you in the bar." But at the German church, lots of people have offered to buy me a beer.
> (Interview conducted on October 11, 2006; Minot, ND)

A second incidence of this disparity regards the older group that Charlie seems to be targeting and the younger age group that is still targeted in much of the Høstfest's advertising. Some good examples of this can be found in a May 2006 advertisement for the Norsk Høstfest from *The Forum*. This twenty-page supplement contains a generous smattering of photos depicting children and young people enjoying various Høstfest activities. The entertainers also seem to be composed largely of young to middle-aged people. And finally, advertised ticket prices are a full fifteen dollars less for thirteen to seventeen-year-olds, while children twelve and under get in free! (This information is courtesy of Dr. Timothy J. Kloberdanz and *The Forum*, May 6, 2006.) It appears that although Charlie may not be interested in targeting the younger members of society, others obviously are.

A third good example of this is found in the official written statement describing the Høstfest. In an excerpt from the Høstfest 2006 Official Festival Guide, Høstfest president Chester Reiten has stated that:

> The foundation of Norsk Høstfest is the celebration of heritage. Heritage is like a lighted torch passed from one generation to the next. It is now up to us, the living, to continue to preserve, enhance, and pass on our heritage. (2006:1)

The Norsk Høstfest is similarly described in most literature that is available to date. I went into this interview with expectations of hearing the same flowery rhetoric from Charlie. What I got was a much more realistic rendition:

> It's semi show business. We use the entertainment to draw them here, but it's a festival. The average person stays three and a half days—this isn't a concert, they don't walk in and then go home. The average daily stay is about eight hours within those three and a half days. If you're going to come in from Regina, Canada, you're not just going to drive down and then go back, you're going to stay for a while. They enjoy it, they're all happy, and most of them are pleased. You can't please everybody, but you do the best you can. You hear very little complaint, and I survey them all the time, about the talent, you know, and what they like and don't like about it. But that's part of show business. (Interview 10/12/06)

From this point on, Charlie went into great detail about the business side of the festival. He talked about target groups, and what different people expected and how to get them to come. He then delved into the realm of discretionary income, highlighting the specific nature of people's spending habits. Finally, we talked economics, specifically Høstfest economics:

> ...We can't lose money you know, there's no home office. This isn't a franchise. We can't call Denver, you know. This is just

> us....We make all the decisions....Show business is the most risky
> business....[Høstfest] is a private, non-profit business.

The Norsk Høstfest, like any other event of this kind, possesses a de-
cidedly business-like aspect that the casual observer might easily over-
look. This may sound cold and non-folkloric, and in some ways it is,
but this festival has to turn a profit in order to remain the independent
entity that it is. I do not by any means imply that because the Høstfest
has this sort of economic aspect it should somehow be considered less
of a folk festival. The Norsk Høstfest does not receive tax money in any
form, according to Charlie, and so it needs to be self-reliant. A lot of
local pride is involved, and this is especially evident in the hoards of
volunteers, most of whom are locals. Minot has earned bragging rights
on account of this festival, and it is the envy of some of the much larger
cities in North Dakota.

The magazine *North Dakota Horizons* ran a recent article on the Norsk
Høstfest with a headline that has been echoed throughout many other publications. In this particular piece, Minot writer Candi Helseth introduces
the article with the words, "Minot steals the show with country's premier
Scandinavian festival" (Fall 2006:9). This statement highlights Minot's
noteworthiness, and how others want a piece of the action. Charlie was
quick to bring this up in our interview:

> ...People wonder, well, how do you do it? Well, we don't tell
> them. Fargo tries it, Grand Forks tries it, there's nobody that can
> do it. They sit here eight deep trying to figure it out....Did you
> see the article in the paper that said "Minot stole the show?"
> Okay, well that says they're all trying it, and it's not working!...
> They all try it, but they're all supported by tax money, so if it
> doesn't work, they say, "Oh, look at all the people we brought
> in." We can't do that, we have to make money.

According to Charlie and other Minot natives I have interviewed, the
Norsk Høstfest is a source of great pride among residents. This unique
festival commands an international reputation and draws more than fifty-
thousand visitors from the United States, Canada, and Europe. The fact
that Minot residents are especially proud of the Høstfest is evidenced
by the hoards of volunteers who donate their time and skills each year.
Charlie emphasized the vital role that volunteers play at the festival:

> We've got seven-thousand volunteers, and a volunteer is differ-
> ent. See, if you are paid for a job, you get paid whether you like
> the job or not. A volunteer is there only because he or she wants
> to be there....You see those guys with the red coats [greeters]

out there (gesturing)? They're out there saying, "Hi, welcome to Minot, thanks for coming, how can I help you?" Well, people like that you know, and all [the volunteers] are proud of Minot, they're proud of the Høstfest, and they're proud of themselves. Otherwise, they wouldn't be a volunteer.

Charlie asserts that Minot comes together as a community each year to make the Høstfest a success. There is a certain synergy that results when people come together en masse, and this stokes the Høstfest engine. It is a competitive enterprise, and many people are envious of the status the little city of Minot enjoys. According to Charlie, it is sometimes quite a struggle to maintain and defend this reputation:

It's a community business. Minot in general is fighting hard. It's a smaller town. We don't have the big four-lane highways; we don't have the big universities. So, we're like the Norwegians, we band together....We gotta fight for our right to be here. That's what the "Minot stole the show" is all about.

I wondered to what extent tourism and the mass media has influenced the festival.

Charlie replied:

It's a media event. My background is in radio and TV. We sell it [Høstfest] by the media. We have one of the top one-hundred destinations in the nation for bus tours. You won't see that within four-hundred miles of here....The mass media, that was me. I owned the radio and TV [stations]. It was the mass media, but I don't come out and say "this is why we're here"—but it is....We do it by advertising. See the first time, the paper had two small pictures of the Høstfest, but then year after year, we did it by commercials....If you look at the radio and TV, it's just loaded [with ads for the Norsk Høstfest] in this area....We use it [the mass media] very extensively. We've got about 250,000 brochures, we're on all the radio stations, all the TV stations, and we're on all the billboards....We use the mass media, because that's my background.

Tourism has become an increasingly important part of Høstfest every year. One good example of this, which I have already mentioned, is Juven Tours of Fargo. This company has a strong presence at the festival, and does a great deal of business there every year. The tourism aspect of Høstfest really is a reciprocal phenomenon. It functions as an exchange program, of sorts, between the United States and Scandinavia.

The festival draws people from the Scandinavian countries, and they then get to know Americans and Canadians at the festival. Oftentimes, these friendships help initiate travel, sending Americans and Canadians over to visit their Scandinavian friends. Many people in the United States and Canada have relatives who live in Scandinavia. The Høstfest can serve as a good context for visiting relatives and even having family reunions. Perhaps the most common way the festival initiates tourism is by reviving interest in heritage, which often results in the desire to visit ancestral homelands. However you care to look at it, the Norsk Høstfest has a very symbiotic relationship with the tourism industry.

The RV is possibly the best, and certainly the most obvious, symbol of tourism at the Høstfest. According to Charlie:

> Tourism is getting bigger. The RVs are here. There's a woman here from Connecticut who interviewed me, you know, it's all over....Go out and look at them [all the RVs], that's *tourism*! You can drive down and look at where all those RVs are from. Two-thirds of them come from a hundred to a thousand miles away. This is moving out.

Business, money, and tourism seem to be as much a part of Høstfest as heritage, culture, and tradition. This factor has created some complex issues. The issues that have arisen throughout all the research and have culminated in this interview have given rise to one burning question: "Is the Norsk Høstfest an authentic folk festival or not?" This question is very problematic for one chief reason—the term "authentic" is extremely relative. Many purists would perhaps say that the Høstfest is not authentic, because it is a staged, manipulated event used to generate money, which afterwards offers a safe return to mainstream life. This assessment has some validity, but it is incomplete. The Norsk Høstfest is highly commercialized, no question, but that is the nature of society today. For a folk festival to be fully successful in this day and age, it must integrate the models of face-to-face community with the realities of an increasingly mobile and globalized society. The Høstfest succeeds in doing this. Another paramount reason the Høstfest is successful, and can be considered an "authentic" folk festival, is that it fulfills its cultural obligations. According to Charlie:

> The basis [of the Høstfest] is for culture....We're here to promote, and preserve, and pass on our culture to the next generation. If we don't do that, this thing will finally fade out and die...it's the underpinning of it, and it impresses some people and not others....This is a unique festival, and there's a reason for it. One of the reasons of it is the higher purpose—the celebration of culture.

The final question I asked Charlie is the same one I have asked many of my other informants: "What makes a good Norwegian?" For the most part, I received the same generic responses I had already heard from most of the others. The main difference is that after naming some chief Norwegian-American attributes, Charlie explained how and why he thought they came about:

> They've got strong family life, strong heritage, they're industrious, you know, they're hard workers, and have good work ethic. And that's true of the Swedes, and of the Germans too. It isn't just the Norwegians that have it, but they're a strong ethnic group—the strongest ethnic group in the country. Norwegians like being Norwegian....If you want to go into history...they were dominated by Denmark for four-hundred years, and then by Sweden, and the Norwegians didn't get free until 1905. Because there was heavy domination, they tended to have to get along to oppose it....Their ethnicity is stronger than most of the others, because the culture I think came about through being dominated by outside powers for so long.

I agree with this final statement very strongly. It makes perfect sense that being dominated by outside powers for many long years would help to solidify Norwegian culture and cause them to value freedom so greatly. Roalson and Liffring-Zug Bourret have referred to Norwegians as "children of freedom....The institutions and the manners of democracy came naturally to them" (2003:23). I assert that it was this great love for freedom and equality that has made the Norwegians such an ideal immigrant group in America, and has helped them to assimilate so successfully.

The fieldwork at the 2006 Norsk Høstfest has been very revealing and has reinforced many of my assertions time and time again. The primary assertion that I have endeavored to establish throughout this study is that the Norsk Høstfest is a symbol of Norwegian-American culture. I am confident that this claim is a very valid one indeed. The Norsk Høstfest is a microcosm of the larger Norwegian-American culture in the Upper Midwest because it celebrates all those cherished attributes that have come to characterize all that is Norwegian American.

Another major assertion that this fieldwork fully supports is the Høstfest's marked relevance to contemporary cultural issues. Perhaps the most pressing of these issues is the maintenance of cultural identity in the face of the conformatory and pervasive nature of globalization. This factor appears time and again at the festival because maintaining cultural identity is highly valued among Norwegian Americans in the Upper Midwest.

I thoroughly enjoyed being at this festival and experiencing all the good things the Norsk Høstfest has to offer. To say the least, the Høstfest was much more exciting and enjoyable than I had ever anticipated it would be. It seems to have an electric atmosphere that somehow manages to draw everyone in. The more that I have been allowed to participate in the Norsk Høstfest, the more meaningful and the more real it has seemed to become for me. This year I worked in the Scandinavian Kitchen again, but this time I had the opportunity to see what it is like to be a real chef for the day—they even let me wear the hat! (Figure 13). The Norsk Høstfest is one event that has the uncanny capacity to beckon all who attend to not only participate, but even wish to be Norwegian—if only for a few short days.

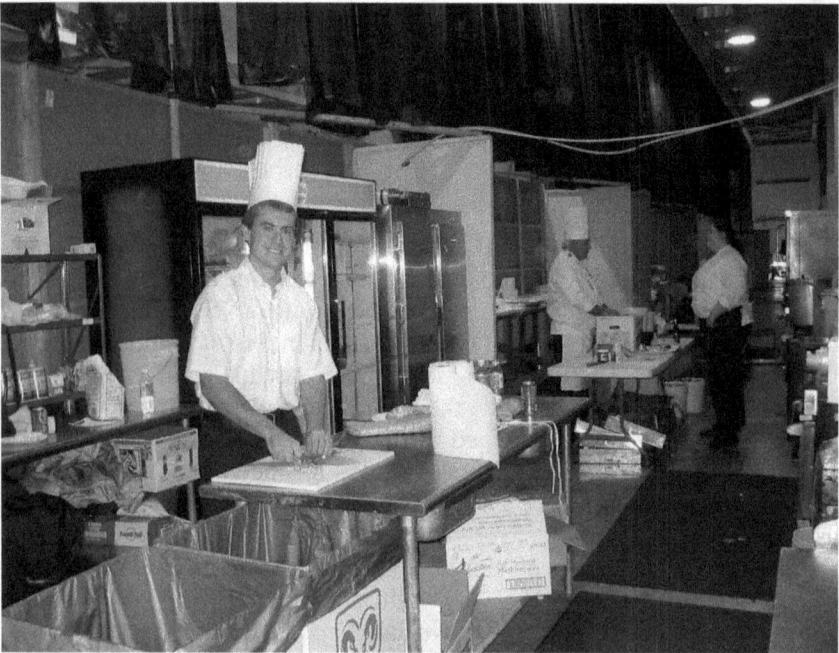

Figure 13. The author doing some cooking at the Scandinavian Kitchen (Photo by Nancy Emch, October 14, 2006; Minot, ND).

Figure 14. The author taking orders at the Scandinavian Kitchen on the final day of the festival (Photo by Nancy Emch, October 14, 2006; Minot, ND).

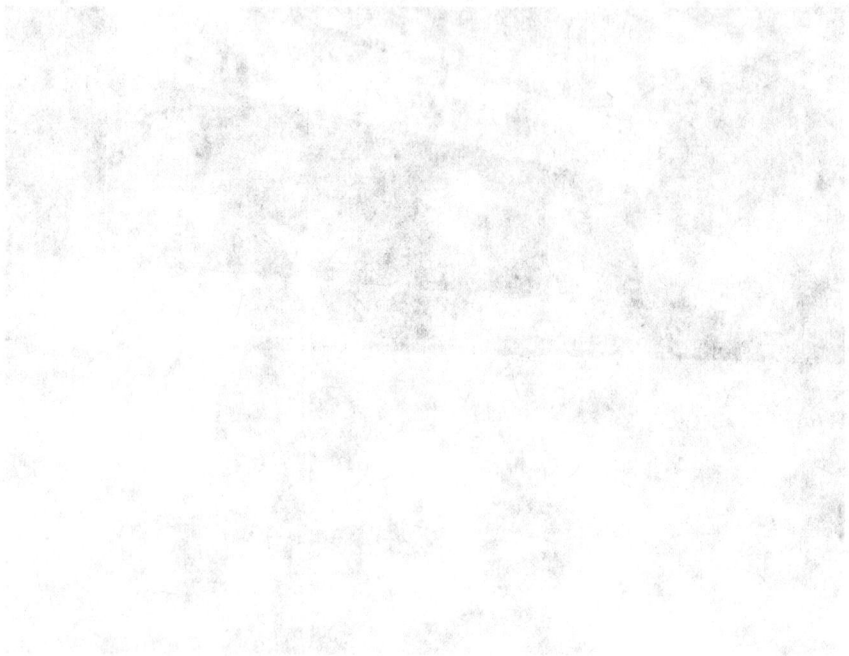

# Summary and Conclusions

It is unfortunate that Charlie's interview did not shed more light on Norwegian-American foodways at the festival. Though several attempts were made to draw him into this area of discussion, he repeatedly returned to those topics with which he was more comfortable. From the very first time I spoke with him over the phone, up to the interview itself, he made it quite clear that the food aspect of the Høstfest was not his specialty, and he had no interest in discussing it. I was happy to learn, however, that many other informants were more than willing to discuss foodways, and so my main assessments regarding foodways have come from them.

I did, nevertheless, manage to get several comments from Charlie relating to Norwegian-American foodways. He did admit that food is an important aspect of the festival and does constitute a major draw. However, he felt that food takes second place to the entertainment, as far as what motivates people to attend the festival. When asked if he thought people would come to the Høstfest solely for the food, he replied, "Everybody thinks they will, but I know they won't" (Interview conducted on October 12, 2006; Minot, ND). Fortunately, however, the vast majority of my informants disagreed with Charlie's assessments about the importance of food, and they assert that it is of vast significance, both within the festival as well as within the broader scope of Norwegian-American culture.

Charlie's tendency to marginalize the role of Norwegian-American food at the festival was regrettable, and at times, somewhat baffling. If the Høstfest is truly about the preservation of Norwegian-American heritage, and if that is "the underpinning of it" that makes it work as Charlie claims, then what part can the big-name entertainers who have little or nothing to do with Norwegian-American heritage really play in this sense? I submit that the entertainment at the festival does play an important role, but not to the extent that Charlie suggests it does. Mike Nelson makes a clear and valid point in stating that "although entertainment often brings people to the festival the first time, the pleasure of getting together and celebrating heritage keeps them coming back, and food is a key ingredient in that celebration" (Olson 1995:51).

It is important to bear in mind that at times the full magnitude of the influence food has on a group is less likely to be recognized by its members. Many times, anthropological analysis of foodways can be very difficult. The average community member often lacks the capacity to recognize or articulate the underlying significance of their own foodways; thus, the process of enculturation is thorough and its effects become deeply ingrained. Because of this, members of a group do not always recognize these meanings and premises when they are stated explicitly, due in large part to the subliminal qualities of culture.

Festivals, which are mass spectacles and cultural performances, provide an ideal means of assessing a community's symbolic, economic, social, and political life. They are especially useful to researchers when they are organized and presented by community members for other community members. Nevertheless, these spectacles also provide an avenue for outsiders to receive the message being presented by the community involved in the celebration. In this way, the Norsk Høstfest affords a glimpse into what matters most to Norwegian Americans. I maintain that The Norsk Høstfest serves an interpretive function. To draw once again from Geertz, it is a Norwegian-American rendition of the Norwegian-American experience, "...a story they tell to themselves about themselves" (1973:448). As anthropologist and ethnographer Philip Carl Salzman has written:

> ...The study of events is particularly useful in the attempt to understand human beings and their lives. Events arise from what people do and are what happens to them. By examining particular events we are able to focus on the specific ways in which people's real lives are expressed, advanced, enhanced, distorted, disrupted, and terminated. This is why I argue that the study of events is the anthropology of real life. (1999:100)

It is true that people make statements about themselves—what they believe in, stand for, admire, and especially what they aspire to be—through events such as festivals. The Norsk Høstfest serves as an ideal setting for displaying cultural identity because it is a performance of what it means to be Norwegian American.

As I have suggested previously, and will now assert in greater detail, the Norsk Høstfest was and still is very timely. The opposition between the forces of localization and globalization was a pressing issue at the beginning of the Høstfest era, and in part the festival arose to address this issue. But this contention between the local and the global has not gone away—rather it has increased. Thus the Høstfest is still very viable in this sense. I assert that Charlie is correct in his assessment that the success of the Høstfest has had much to do with its opportune timing. Charlie has stated, "There's nothing more powerful than an idea whose time has come. It was time for a celebration of ethnicity, and it went up" (Interview conducted on October 12, 2006; Minot, ND).

Globalization, though it brings great change with it, is a good and necessary thing. It is of crucial importance to the Upper Midwest as well as the rest of the nation, and most people in the Upper Midwestern United States seem to recognize this. Oftentimes, however, globalization brings with it cultural change and so resistance to it is to be expected.

The persistence of Norwegian-American culture should by no means be looked down on or viewed in any other derogatory way. An entirely homogeneous society would certainly be a very bland and unfruitful one. Points of cultural common ground are important in society, but so are differences—the two compliment each other. Those things that set other cultures apart are important, because in essence, that is exactly what culture is all about—the points by which one group distinguishes itself from another. Cultural distinction, or more specifically belongingness, can then be seen as an indispensable human need; because in terms of heritage, the past does help bring meaning and guidance to the present. In Norwegian-American culture, where quiet defiance of cultural change would seem to be the norm, the Norsk Høstfest exists to display more overt, yet culturally appropriate forms of this defiance.

According to Canadian anthropologist Carole Farber, festivals are about identity, "whether individual or collective." They represent the context and the process for creating links between people in the community, as well as between the community and the wider national and international cultural environments (1983:33–42). In this way, the Norsk Høstfest is an exceptional medium for addressing the complex issues surrounding the anxiety produced by the clash of globalization and localization in the Upper Midwest. I assert, as I have alluded to above, that there exists an apprehension in the Upper Midwest associated with change. More specifically, Norwegian Americans fear losing their culture, of which they are very proud. This is one important reason why festivals such as the Norsk Høstfest exist—to address and calm such fears. According to

Jackie, the college student who has also spent some time doing research at the Høstfest for a paper, "[Traditional Norwegian culture] is so rigid. People are so afraid of losing it, that they want to keep it exactly intact" (Interview conducted on March 23, 2006; Fargo, ND). Mrs. Olson, speaking about the fear of change and how it affects both the Høstfest and the Sons of Norway Lodge, states:

> ...If we lose this, if the younger generations don't want to take it up, we're gonna lose it....It's like I said, the culture is trying to keep up, but you can't live it anymore, life has changed, you know. The Norwegians have changed, even over there in Norway, they have changed, especially the younger generation, they have changed a lot, they're getting more Americanized all the time. (Interview conducted on April 6, 2006; Fargo, ND)

Mr. Olson piped in with his own qualms about the resistance to change that he himself has witnessed at their own Sons of Norway Lodge:

> That's the trouble we've got here, we can't change nothing, because...see that wall (gestures), that's sacred, you don't wanna mess with that (mockingly). You can't get 'em to change *nothing*. We had a nice border picked out for around the ceiling, to lower it you know, but it said made in China on it, so the one guy said, "Can't use it." If you could order it out of Norway, then we could use it.

This anxiety brought about by the fear of change has been a constantly recurring theme in this study, and one that has been echoed by many informants both young and old. The world is becoming more and more globalized, and that is a source of worry for a lot of people. Festivals like the Høstfest, however, exist as a safe environment where the local and the global can coexist for a time and the old traditions can be upheld.

Spencer R. Crew and James E. Sims assert that there are many ways in which a festival or celebration can assist in crossing boundaries between cultures and communities. More so than in a static exhibition, the audience or participants in a festival take part in the spatial temporality of the event and become "co-creators of social meaning" (1991:174).

Indeed, festival times are those in which out-of-the-ordinary things can and do happen. It is a time when the social norms of everyday life are somehow less of a factor. The renowned anthropologist Victor Turner points out that the festival is "a place which is no place and a time which is no time" (1983:103). The study of events can give the anthropologist very useful tools for the understanding of culture because festivals can bring to the forefront certain important aspects of culture that are otherwise not addressed in everyday life. Festivals like the Norsk Høstfest are a means by which people can and do showcase those things that matter most to them as human beings. When asked about why people keep coming back to the Norsk Høstfest, Lester said:

> It's culture. I mean, I think that's the hook, is to draw you into your past, into your memories, or into a new experience that you have an interest in. You can always say, well, I was different, but you're always kind of comparing it against...what you came from, or from what you thought. So, that's why I think people come. Because it wouldn't always be for just quality of entertainment, I don't think. (Interview conducted April 29, 2006; Grand Forks, ND)

This study has demonstrated time and again the means by which traditional foodways are used within contemporary Norwegian-American culture to convey meaning. One of the primary messages that food helps to express is acceptance. Lester shared the biblical story of Zacchaeus (a tax collector who by the cultural standards of his time was an outcast, a person with whom others did not willingly associate) to emphasize this point:

> In Jesus' time, when he went to eat with Zacchaeus, I think that was a very significant thing, it wasn't that he just went and visited with him, he ate, and fellowshipped with him. It was a sign of an acceptance, not only of the host—it was a sign of recognition or acknowledgement of who they are.

Food possesses the unique potential for communicating both acceptance of others, and acceptance by others. Since numerous informants have listed hospitality and warmth as major attributes of Norwegian-American culture throughout this study, it is only natural that food should serve as the chief conveyor of this sentiment. One has but to observe the Høstfest briefly in order to see the importance of this theme there. The thematic statements printed in the Høstfest 2005 and 2006 Official Festival Guides, for example, bear this out. Festival attendees are presented with such slogans as "Share the warmth of Norsk Høstfest" (Høstfest 2005 Official Festival Guide), and "There's no place like Høstfest" (Høstfest 2006 Official Festival Guide).

The overall significance of foodways within Norwegian-American culture is incalculably vast, because foodways are so completely integrated into the culture. Foodways serve as a primary means for asserting cultural identity, because food, unlike most other cultural markers, is something that we all use and rely on daily. Foodways are exceptional among other symbolic media, because they seem to be the most culturally acceptable means for declaring cultural identity in the Upper Midwestern United States. As Marie, a former NDSU student asserts:

> In my family we don't speak the language [Norwegian], and never have. We don't go to Norway, and we don't dress Norwegian. None of those things are really practical....Wearing clothing like that would almost set you apart too much I think. Food though, is practical, and it's something you're still gonna do. That's why *lefse* is the one thing we still hold on to. (Interview conducted on November 5, 2006; Fargo, ND)

If there is one thing that this study has made clear, it is that foodways persist where all other means for declaring cultural solidarity diminish. Norwegian Americans have a great deal of pride in their heritage, but since overt declarations of pride constitute unacceptable behavior, that pride is channeled and filtered through foodways. Norwegian-American foodways function as the shared cultural symbols that help bind the group together and distinguish them from other cultures. In this way, Norwegian-American foodways point to a cultural system of meaning that is made manifest at the Norsk Høstfest.

Coming to understand Norwegian-American foodways and culture in the Upper Midwest has been a daunting task. However, the Norsk Høstfest truly has proven to be an ideal event for analysis in this endeavor. Through careful examination of this festival, it has become quite apparent that the adaptability of Norwegian-American culture is a major theme with great implications. This adaptability may well be one of the chief reasons Norwegian Americans were and are so successful in this part of the Northern Great Plains.

The examination of which foodways have been altered or influenced by local conditions and factors has been quite useful to this study. In assessing the formation and current structure of Norwegian-American foodways, the investigation as to why certain types of food have come about at all has proven to be very revealing. Whether it is the ease of preparation, the existence of plentiful ingredients, or the utility of the type of food, surroundings do have a great effect on foodways. Nikki Bado-Fralick, who specializes in women's studies and religious studies, states that the Great Plains settlers were "make do" people and adapted to local conditions (2004:313). The theme of adaptability has surfaced time and time again throughout this study. It has proven to be both a formative force and a noble attribute in the Norwegian-American experience. This adaptability is perhaps best represented in the realm of foodways, as documented exclusively throughout this project. Many changes have been made to

Norwegian foods in the U.S. that correspond sharply to pressure from local factors.

Adaptability is especially mirrored in Norwegian-American foodways,
because their culture, like other cultures, is so closely associated with
food. Since food does have this intimate link with culture, people seem to
be able to relate well to it within the context of a festival. In this way, the
Høstfest uses food to draw people in and communicate a variety of messages with great success. Given that food seems to be the most effective
medium for transmitting universal generic messages within culture, and
that the Norsk Høstfest is so inextricably linked with foodways, it is no
wonder the festival is as successful as it is.

The Norsk Høstfest is a very successful festival, and it does have a
great impact on those who are involved in it. One major reason for this
is that the festival appeals to many different people, not just Norwegian
Americans. Although Norwegian-American culture is indeed a major
theme at the festival, it attracts many different types of people. As Charlie
pointed out to me as he gestured, "That's the general population of North
Dakota out there in that room." The Norsk Høstfest is equally relevant to
Upper Midwesterners and other Americans alike, because it reminds us of
our common social history of immigration. America is a nation composed
largely of immigrants, and this festival is an excellent venue for that sentiment to be acknowledged as well as celebrated.

The question of the "authenticity" of the festival has come up again and
again, and there is one final aspect of this question that needs to be addressed, no matter how difficult it may be. That is the question of whether
or not the Norsk Høstfest is an "authentic" folk festival. This study will
put forth no lists of characteristics with which to judge the legitimacy of
this festival, simply because, as argued above, culture is a process and
cannot be properly understood through lists of quantifiable traits. The
case for "authenticity" then is built on the simple assertion that the Norsk
Høstfest fulfills the needs of those who attend it. Many, perhaps most of
those who attend, are Scandinavian Americans.

The verdict is simple; people enjoy themselves at the festival, they love
it, and they come back for more year after year, usually bringing others
with them. So in this sense, the Norsk Høstfest is "authentic." Also, the
vast body of volunteers who come to donate their time and efforts every
year are another great indication of "authenticity." The presence of so
many volunteers at the festival bears witness to the fact that though these
individuals do not receive any monetary compensation, they obviously
gain some substantial benefits from their time at the festival. Many of the
volunteers at the Høstfest are local residents who take great pride in the

fact that Minot is so well-known across the United States because of the Høstfest. In this way, local Minot volunteers have the opportunity to serve as ambassadors and promoters of their city.

However, this phenomenon is not limited solely to Minot residents; it is not a feeling or an experience that applies only to "insiders" and is somehow lost on others. I argue that to be a volunteer at the Norsk Høstfest is to be an insider. It is the fast track to feeling accepted and having a real, tangible reason for being there, especially when you do not quite fit in with the predominantly elderly crowd, as was the case for me. There is an atmosphere of inclusiveness and synergy in the Hostfest that appeals to people, and motivates them to participate. This force, which could be termed the "festival factor," is the real engine that drives the Høstfest, and it is particularly embodied in the vast volunteer force at the festival. When people are caught up in a large-scale collective effort like the Hostfest, they become part of something bigger than themselves. This constitutes authenticity in its purest form.

Finally, how do we define "authenticity"? It seems presumptuous to consider labeling this festival a fake due to its commercialization, or any other factor for that matter. To do so would mean we are implying that people who attend the festival have somehow been hoodwinked into believing some colossal lie. As Marie asserts:

> It's authentic to our present culture, since our culture is so commercialized. Sure it's about making money, and I think most people who go there understand that, but there is something authentic at the core of it. There's something authentic about it that people can relate to; otherwise it would not be so successful. (Interview conducted on November 5, 2006; Fargo, ND)

So, upon close examination of this festival, and in light of the factors enumerated above, the question as to whether the Høstfest is "authentic" or not effectively loses value. It would seem that only a passing glance assessment could result in the Norsk Høstfest being labeled as anything but the genuine folk festival that it is.

Some would suggest that the Norsk Høstfest is mired in the past and that when those who attend it—mostly senior citizens—are dead and gone, the festival, too, will fade out and die. This may very well be true. It is a very real truth that anything that is unwilling or unable to adapt to its environment will eventually wither and die. This is true in the physical world of organisms, and it seems true in the cultural realm of festival as well. Festivals must continually be integrating new cultural inputs into what already exists. If festivals are not able to blend the old with the new and do not submit to the changing nature of culture, they will cease to exist. Beverly J. Stoeltje, who has addressed the extensive role of festival within culture, writes:

> Substance in festival derives from traditions based on common identity; thus festival emphasizes the past. Yet festival occurs in and for the present; thus social change emerges. Specifically, if contemporary themes and styles are not incorporated in festival, it fails quickly, but if the traditional substance becomes lost, the festival dies with the passing of the contemporary. This process then constitutes a dimension of human action where two temporal realities, the past and the present, function in tandem. (1983:240)

Upon close examination and extensive study, it seems unlikely that the Norsk Høstfest will suffer such a fate. This festival seems to maintain a delicate balance between the traditional and the modern, the local and the global. As to the concern that the Høstfest will die out with the passing of its mostly elderly attendees, this too, appears to be rather unlikely. The Høstfest will certainly change, but it will most likely not die out. As Charlie points out, most of the people who took part in the Høstfest in its early years are long gone. If his assertion that people become more interested in their heritage as they get into their fifties and "come up," then this festival is in no immediate danger of dying out. The fact that the Norsk Høstfest has grown rapidly over the years, rather than diminishing, gives further credibility to this assertion.

The Norsk Høstfest is a performance and a celebration, and above all, a symbol of what it means to be Norwegian American. Examining traditional foodways within the framework of this annual and very popular ethnic festival keenly supports this concept. Culture directs and influences our actions as human beings, and it works in our lives like a subconscious playbook. It guides our actions as social creatures, often without our even being aware of its subtle and pervasive power. By applying Geertz's interpretive theory, the Norsk Høstfest emerges as a vital means by which the Norwegian-American journey is celebrated and even relived. In the continually changing world of today, in which the forces of globalization exert so much pressure on cultures to conform, the Norsk Hostfest represents a means by which Norwegian-American cultures can be celebrated–and preserved for posterity.

# Glossary of Norwegian and Non-English Terms

*Bannock*—a type of baked skillet bread, similar to a scone, introduced by the Scots and prepared traditionally from flour, lard, water, and baking powder (Woolf 1999:25).

*Berlinerkranser*—"Berlin Wreaths," a type of cookie (Forlag 1995:217).

*Bunad*—a festive costume traditionally worn in Norway and continued in America (Roalson and Liffring-Zug Bourret 2003:6–7).

*Får i kål*—"Lamb and cabbage stew" (Forlag 1995:6).

*Fiskeboller*—"Fish balls" (Roalson and Liffring-Zug Bourret 2003:82).

*Fiskepudding*—A baked mixture of flaked fish and cream sauce (Roalson and Liffring-Zug Bourret 2003:82).

*Fiskesuppe*—"Fish soup" (Roalson and Liffring-Zug Bourret 2003:6–7).

*Fattigmann*—"Poor Man's Cookies" (Forlag 1995:207).

*Gravlaks*—Uncooked, marinated salmon that is served chilled in very thin slices (Roalson and Liffring-Zug Bourret 2003:87).

*Grøt*—"Porridge," the hearty porridge made by boiling milk with flour (Roalson and Liffring-Zug Bourret 2003:81).

*Kransekake*—Ring or tree (cake) is a festival tradition in Norway (Roalson and Liffring-Zug Bourret 2003:131).

*Krumkake*—"Cones," a type of cookie baked in an iron, rolled into a cone shape, and then cooled (Forlag 1995:209).

*Langskip*—"Long ship," a type of ship used by the Vikings (The Sons of Norway Songbook 1948:1).

*Larder*—A storehouse where food was traditionally kept in Norway (Forlag 1995:23).

*Lefse*—a type of flat bread usually made with potatoes and baked on a griddle (Forlag 1995:211-216).

*Lutefisk*—Dried codfish that is soaked in lye for preservation and later reconstituted in boiling water to make it palatable (Forlag 1995:12–14).

*Muelter*—rare yellow berries that grow wild on mountain plateaus in Norway (Roalson and Liffring-Zug Bourret 2003:87).

*Nissen*—a benevolent elf featured in Norwegian folklore (Vanberg 1970:82).

*Nykelharpa*—a traditional Swedish stringed instrument (Høstfest 2006 Souvenir Magazine).

*Pålegg*—"Something put on bread" (Forlag 1995:6).

*Rømmegrøt*—"Sour Cream Porridge" (Roalson and Liffring-Zug Bourret 2003:62). *Rosemaling*—Decorative painting that is possibly the best-known form of Norwegian folk art (Roalson and Liffring-Zug Bourret 2003:75).

*Rosettbakkels*—"Rosettes," a type of Norwegian cookie that is thin and hollow (Forlag 1995:208).

*Rullepølse*—"Rolled, pressed sandwich meat" (Roalson and Liffring-Zug Bourret 2003:95).

*Spekemat*—"Cured dried meat" (Roalson and Liffring-Zug Bourret 2003:87).

*Syttende Mai*—"May Seventeenth," Norway's Constitution Day (Vanberg 1970:77).

# References

Appadurai, Arjun, ed. 1986. *The social life of things: Commodities in cultural perspective*. New York: Cambridge University Press.

Appadurai, Arjun. 1990. Disjuncture and difference in the global cultural economy. In M. Featherstone (ed.), *Global culture: Nationalism, globalization, and modernity*, 295–310. London: Sage.

Bado-Fralick, Nikki. 2004. Seasonal celebrations. In David J. Wishart (ed.), *Encyclopedia of the Great Plains*, 313. Lincoln: University of Nebraska Press.

Barth, Fredrik. 1969. *Ethnic groups and boundaries*. Boston: Little, Brown, and Co.

Barthes, Roland. 1997. Towards a psychosociology of contemporary food consumption. In Carole M. Counihan and Penny Van Esterik (eds.), *Food and culture: A reader*, 202–208. New York: Routledge.

Bass, M. A., L. M. Wakefield, and K. M. Kolassa. 1979. *Community nutrition and individual food behavior*. Minneapolis, Minnesota: Burgess Publishing.

Brown, Linda Keller and Kay Mussell. 1984. *Ethnic and regional foodways in the United States*. Knoxville: University of Tennessee Press.

Charsley, Simon R. 1992. *Wedding cakes and cultural history*. London: Routledge.

Cohen, Abner. 1944. *Two dimensional man: An essay on the anthropology of power and symbolism in complex society*. Berkeley: University of California Press.

Counihan, Carole M. 1999. The social and cultural uses of food. In Kenneth F. Kiple and Conee Kriemhild Ornelas-Kipple (eds.), *The Cambridge world history of food and nutrition*, 20–114. New York: Cambridge University Press.

Crew, Spencer R. and James E. Sims. 1991. Locating authenticity: Fragments of a dialogue. In Ivan Karp and Steven D. Levine (eds.), *Exhibiting cultures: The poetics and politics of museum display*, 159–175. Washington, D.C.: Smithsonian Institution Press.

Des Chene, Mary. 1996. Symbolic anthropology. In David Levinson and Melvin Ember (eds.), *Encyclopedia of cultural anthropology*, 1274–1278. New York: Henry Holt & Co.

Dolgin, Janet, David Kemnitzer, and David Schneider, eds. 1977. *Symbolic anthropology: A reader in the study of symbols and meanings*. New York: Columbia Press.

Douglas, Mary. 1972. Deciphering a meal. In Clifford Geertz (ed.), *Myth, symbol, and culture*, 61–81. New York: Norton.

Douglas, Mary. 1975. *Implicit meanings: Essays in anthropology*. London: Routledge & Keagan Paul, Ltd.

DuPuis, Melanie E. 2002. *Nature's perfect food: How milk became America's drink*. New York: New York University Press.

Erdman, Aimee. December 2005. A cure for boredom: Minot thinks big. *Prairie Business Magazine*, Fargo, North Dakota. Retrieved March 24, 2006 from http://www.prairiebizmag.com/article.asp?id = 892.

Eriksen, Thomas Hylland. 1994. Milk as a symbol of Norwegianness. *Norway Now*. Retrieved February, 2006 from http://folk.uio.no/geirthe/Milk.html.

Farber, Carole. 1983. High, healthy and happy: Ontario mythology on parade. In Frank E. Manning (ed.), *The Celebration of society: Perspectives on contemporary cultural performance*, 33–42. Bowling Green, Ohio: Popular Press.

Fieldhouse, Paul. 1986. *Food & nutrition: Customs & culture*. New York: Croom Helm and Methuen, Inc.

*Forum, The*. Fargo, North Dakota. Thursday, 13 October 2005: P. A11.

*Forum, The*. Fargo, North Dakota. Thursday, 12 October 2006: P. A11.

*Forum, The*. Fargo, North Dakota. Saturday, 6 May 2006: Special Norsk Høstfest insert, pp. 1–19.

Gallini, Clara. 1971. *Il consumo del sacro: Feste Lunghe de Sardegna*. Bari, Italy: Laterza.

Geertz, Clifford. 1973. *The interpretation of cultures: Selected essays*. New York: Basic Books.

Gifft, H. H., M. B. Washbon, and C. G. Harrison. 1972. *Nutrition, behavior, and change*. New Jersey: Prentice Hall.

Gillespie, Angus Kress. 1996. Festival. In Jan Harold Brunvand (ed.), *American folklore: An encyclopedia*, 249–252. New York: Garland Publishing.

Gofton, Leslie. 1986. The rules of the table. In Christopher Ritson, Leslie Gofton, and John McKenzie (eds.), *The food consumer*, 127–153. New York: John Wiley & Sons.

Goody, Jack. 1982. *Cooking, cuisine and class: A study in comparative sociology*. Cambridge: Cambridge University Press.

Hansen, Marcus Lee. 1940. *The immigrant in American history*. Cambridge, Massachusetts: Harvard University Press.

Helseth, Candi. 2006. Three decades of Høstfest: Minot steals the show with country's premier Scandinavian Festival. In *North Dakota Horizons*. 36(4):9–13.

Høstfest 2005 Official festival guide. Minot, North Dakota: Creative Printing.

Høstfest 2006 Official festival guide. Minot, North Dakota: Creative Printing.

Høstfest 2006 Souvenir magazine. Jo Ann Winistorfer, ed. (assisted by Norsk Hostfest staff members). Photos from Hostfest archives.

Inter Tran website. Retrieved January, 2006 from http://www.tranexp.com:2000/Translate/result.shtml.

Jerome, N.W. 1970. American culture and food habits. In Jacqueline Dupont (ed.), *Dimensions of nutrition*, 32–45. Boulder, Colorado: Colorado Associated University Press.

Kloberdanz, Timothy J. (Instructor). 2006. "Germans from Russia" Course. Anthropology 461/661. North Dakota State University, Fargo, North Dakota. Spring semester 2006.

KOM Forlag. 1995. *The Norwegian kitchen*, Kjell Innli, ed. Boston: Skandisk, Inc.

Legwold, Gary. 1992. *The last word on lefse*. Cambridge, Minnesota: Adventure Publications.

Letnes Martin, Janet, and Suzann (Johnson) Nelson. 1994. *Cream peas on toast: Comfort food for Norwegian-Lutheran farm kids (and others)*. Hastings, Minnesota: Caragana Press.

Letnes Martin, Janet, and Suzann (Johnson) Nelson. 1997. *Growing up Lutheran: What does this mean?* Hastings, Minnesota: Caragana Press.

Lévi Strauss, Claude. 1966. The culinary triangle. *Partisan Review*. 33(4):586–595.

Local Legacies website. Retrieved November, 2005 from http://www.loc.gov/bicentennial/legacies.html.

Magliocco, Sabina. 2006. *The two Madonnas: The politics of festival in a Sardinian community.* 2nd ed. Long Grove, Illinois: Waveland Press, Inc.

Manning, F. E. 1983. Cosmos and chaos: Celebration in the modern world. In F. E. Manning (ed.), *The celebration of society: Perspectives on contemporary cultural performance,* 3–32. Bowling Green: Bowling Green University Press.

Marzolf, Arnold H. 1995. *That's the way it once was* [So hen mers amohl kaht]: *Black Sea Germans from Russia experiences.* Bismarck, North Dakota: Germans from Russia Heritage Society.

McIntosh, Elaine N. 1995. *American food habits in historical perspective.* Westport, London: Praeger Publishers.

Murcott, Anne. 1986. You are what you eat: Anthropological factors influencing food choice. In Christopher Ritson, Leslie Gofton, and John Mckenzie (eds.), *The food consumer,* 107–125. New York: John Wiley & Sons.

Olson, Lori and Jim Olson. 1995. *Norsk Høstfest: Heritage comes alive.* Helena, Montana: Norsk Høstfest Association and American World Geographic Publishing.

Peterson, Gloria, and Dean Peterson. "The *lutefisk* ritual." For a parody on "A night before Christmas"—as told by a Scandinavian who hates *lutefisk.* Retrieved January 2006, from http://www.lawzone.com/half-nor/lutefisk.htm.

Roalson, Louise and Joan Liffring-Zug Bourret. 2003. *Norwegian touches: Notably Norwegian revised and expanded history, recipes and folk arts.* Iowa City, Iowa: Penfield Books.

Rölvaag, O. E. 1927. *Giants in the earth: A saga of the prairie.* New York: Harper & Row.

Sahlins, Marshall. 1990. Food as symbolic code. In Jeffrey Alexander and Steven Seidman (eds.), *Culture and society: contemporary debates,* 94–101. Cambridge: Cambridge University Press.

Salzman, Philip Carl. 1999. *The anthropology of real life: Events in human experience.* Prospect Heights, Illnois: Waveland Press, Inc.

Sanjur, Diva. 1982. *Social and cultural perspectives in nutrition.* Englewood Cliffs, New Jersey: Prentice Hall.

Sherman, William C. 1983. *Prairie mosaic: An ethnic atlas of rural North Dakota.* Fargo, North Dakota: North Dakota Institute for Regional Studies, North Dakota State University.

Sherman, William C., and Playford V. Thorson, eds. 1988. *Plains folk: North Dakota's ethnic history.* Fargo, North Dakota: North Dakota Institute for Regional Studies, North Dakota State University.

Sons of Norway Supreme Lodge. 1948. *Sons of Norway songs for community singing.* Minneapolis, Minn.: Supreme Lodge Sons of Norway.

Stoeltje, Beverly J. 1983. Festival in America. In Richard M. Dorson (ed.), *Handbook of American folklore,* 239–246. Bloomington: Indiana University Press. *Tales of Minnesota.* 1987. A television documentary. Twin Cities Public TV. St. Paul, Minnesota. A KTCA Program.

Turner, Victor. 1983. Carnival in Rio: Dionysian drama in an industrializing society. In Frank E. Manning (ed.), *The celebration of society: Perspectives on contemporary cultural performance,* 103–114. Bowling Green, Ohio: Popular Press.

Vanberg, Bent. 1970. *Of Norwegian ways.* Minneapolis, Minnesota: Dillon Press.

*Western Viking.* 26 August 2005. Weekly Newspaper. Published in Seattle, Washington. P. 1.

Wiley, Andrea S. 2004. Drink milk for fitness: The cultural politics of human biological variation and milk consumption in the United States. *American Anthropologist* 106(3): 506–517.

Woolf, Nonie. 1999. *Northern Plains Indian food practices, customs, and holidays.* American Dietetic Association: Alexandria, VA.

Zeitlin, Steven J., Amy J. Kotkin, and Holly Cutting Baker. 1982. *A celebration of American family folklore: Tales and traditions from the Smithsonian collection.* New York: Pantheon Books.

SIL International®
The International Museum of Cultures
Publications in Ethnology

Other Publications

40. Our company increases apace: History, language, and social identity in early colonial Andover, Massachucetts, by Elinor Abbot, 2007.
39. What place for hunters-gatherers in millenium three? by Thomas N. Headland and Doris E. Blood, eds. 2002.
38. A tale of Pudicho's people, by Richard Montag. 2002.
37. African friends and money matters, by David E. Maranz, 2001.
36. The value of the person in the Guahibo culture, by Marcelino Sosa, translated by Walter del Aguila, 1999.
35. People of the drums—Come!, by Paul Neeley, 1999.
34. Cashibo folklore and culture: Prose, poetry, and historical background, by Lila Wistrand-Robinson, 1998.
33. Symbolism and ritual in Irian Jaya, Marilyn Gregerson and Joyce Sterner, eds., 1997.
32. Kinship and social organization in Irian Jaya: A glimpse of seven systems, Marilyn Gregerson and Joyce Sterner, eds., 1977.
31. Ritual, belief, and kinship in Sulawesi, by Marilyn Gregerson, ed., 1993.
30. Ritual, and relationships in the Valley of the Sun: The Ketengban of Irian Jaya, by Andrew Sims and Anne Sims, 1992.
29. Not published
28. Peace is everything, by David E. Maranz, 1993.
27. Mice are men: Language and society anong the Murle of Sudan, by Jonathan E. Arensen, 1992.
26. Language choice in rural development, by Clinton D. W. Robinson, 1992.
25. El arte cofan en tejido de hamacas. The Cofan art of hammock weaving, by M. B. Borman, 1992.

For further information or a full listing of SIL publications contact:

SIL International Publications
7500 West Camp Wisdom Road
Dallas, TX 75236-5699

Voice: 972-708-7404
Fax: 972-708-7363
Email: academic_books@sil.org
Internet: http://www.ethnologue.com

www.ingramcontent.com/pod-product-compliance
Lightning Source LLC
Chambersburg PA
CBHW050718280326
41926CB00088B/3259